# HIDDEN HISTORY

### *of*

# MONTGOMERY COUNTY, MARYLAND

# HIDDEN HISTORY

## *of*

# MONTGOMERY COUNTY, MARYLAND

*Brian Myers*

THE
History
PRESS

Published by The History Press
Charleston, SC
www.historypress.com

*Front cover*: Automobiles race down a dirt track at the Rockville Fair, August 1923. The fair was held about where Richard Montgomery High School is currently located. *Library of Congress.*
*Back cover*: When William Beall's 1915 Pullman automobile broke down, his brother Vernon towed him by horseback to Reed Brothers garage to get it fixed. This photo was taken along Veirs Mill Road in Rockville, with St. Mary's Catholic Church in the background. *Photo by Lewis Reed, courtesy of Jeanne Gartner.*

First published 2025

Manufactured in the United States

ISBN 9781467156608

Library of Congress Control Number: 2024947400

*Notice*: The information in this book is true and complete to the best of our knowledge. It is offered without guarantee on the part of the author or The History Press. The author and The History Press disclaim all liability in connection with the use of this book.

# CONTENTS

Preface ................................................................................. 7
Acknowledgements ............................................................. 9

PART I. EARLY MOCO HISTORY
1. A Crash Course in Pre-MoCo History ............................... 13
2. Georgetown College, but Later University, of Maryland,
   but Even Later of Washington, the District of Columbia ................. 20
3. Woodstock: George Washington's Farm That Time Once Forgot ........ 23
4. First There's the Poorhouse, Then There's Prison ........................... 28
5. The Lost Town of Triadelphia ....................................... 32
6. A Bloody Battle, $3,000 Skirts and Other Tales from the Civil War .....36

PART II. CHANGEMAKERS
7. Josiah Henson, Passenger and Conductor on the
   Underground Railroad ............................................... 43
8. Doctor Bird: Sandy Spring's Most Beloved Deliveryman ................... 48
9. Rachel Carson's *Silent Spring* from Silver Spring ........................ 54
10. Go Wildcats! The Story of Clarksburg's Wilson Wims ...................... 57
11. Joe Acanfora vs. MCPS: A Case Study of the
    Gay Rights Movement .............................................. 60
12. The Growth and Strength of MoCo's Jewish Community ............... 67

CONTENTS

PART III. THE OTHER SIDE OF MOCO
13. What a Way to Go: Dramatic Deaths with Crazy Causes.................75
14. A County Full of Ghosts.................80
15. The Tornado That Came to Laytonsville .................84
16. Villainous "Villa" Thompson Blows a Fuse.................90
17. Aspin Hill Pet (and Human) Cemetery .................101

PART IV. ENTERTAINMENT
18. An Amusing History of Glen Echo Park.................109
19. See the Forest for the Trees—and Washington Grove, Too.................116
20. Ladies and Gentlemen, the Cornet Band.................120
21. The Star-Studded Shady Grove Music Fair .................124
22. Billy and Porky, the Trash-Talking Animals.................127
23. A-MoCo-an Horror Story: Behind the Scenes of *The Blair Witch Project* with Eduardo Sánchez and Matt Blazi .................131

PART V. THE COUNTRY AND THE ROADS
24. The Family Tree of Butler's Orchard.................143
25. Turkey Thicket: A Snapshot of Farm Life over One Hundred Years Ago .................150
26. Damascus's Declassified Dinner Recipe Guide.................154
27. It's Not Just the Street You Live On .................159
28. That John Denver Song "Take Me Home, Clopper Road" .................164

PART VI. LESSONS LEARNED
29. The Power of Gold Fever.................169
30. Garrett Park and the Troublesome Toilet .................172
31. The Gaithersburg Latitude Observatory .................176
32. Fifteen Years and Thirty-Two Tall-Grassed Acres of Fourth School .................180
33. Montgomery County Personal Histories: Living over Eighty Years in MoCo .................184

Bibliography.................193
Index .................201
About the Author.................207

# PREFACE

I'm extremely grateful to have grown up in Montgomery County, Maryland, even with a few awkward moments along the way. When I was eleven years old, there were a lot of conversations that went like this:

Me: "My great-grandfather discovered Bessie Smith and Hank Williams!"

A fifth-grade classmate: "Eh? Who?"

At six years old, visiting my grandparents' house, kismet led me to pull a large, unassuming binder from a bookshelf, and I began to study the names, dates and photos that made up what I soon realized was something called a "genealogy." It was a big word for a kindergartener, and I was proud to have learned it.

Toward the end of elementary school—with my parents' permission, of course—I got started on Ancestry.com and began researching more of our family tree. I had already found a lot on my mother's side through her family's genealogy, but I was curious to discover more about my father's side. Mom-Mom, as we called his mother, had Sicilian blood, but I never knew much history about Granddad, his father, other than that we shared the same birthday, September 13.

So I began to look. Dad grew up in Howard County, Maryland. Granddad was from Baltimore. Granddad's mom was from Frederick County, Maryland, I discovered. And before that? Montgomery County, Maryland. Over the course of a century and a half, without realizing it, we came back to our roots, right here in MoCo. We never realized, living in Gaithersburg, that there was a road two neighborhoods down named after the family of Dad's great-uncle Wilson Tschiffely.

In the past twelve years of studying old newspaper clippings, emailing back and forth with distant cousins and putting off algebra homework to visit cemeteries, I've gotten to understand and appreciate every anecdote and hidden bombshell Montgomery County has to offer. I've heard all kinds of local stories. Wedding dresses set on fire? The young doctor credited with saving a town from a deadly epidemic? A community banding together to protect themselves from their neighbor's toilet? Yes, this is really our MoCo.

I am honored to share with you more than thirty hidden historical narratives about Montgomery County, Maryland. Picking which topics to cover was not an easy task. In almost 250 years, we've metamorphosed from having tobacco fields to having train tracks to having one of those car vending machines, where you put in the giant coin and you get back a Ford Mustang.

As I'm writing this, I'm twenty-three years old, and I've become a fanatic for my county's history. It's never too late to find out who you are, and if this process has taught me anything, it's never too early. If this book makes you appreciate MoCo even a little bit more, I'll have done my job right. Enjoy!

# ACKNOWLEDGEMENTS

Thank you to my commissioning editor, Kate Jenkins, for helping me navigate this new and challenging adventure. When I first reached out to Arcadia Publishing about this project, I didn't know who was going to answer on the other end, but I'm so glad it was you. You have always been cheerful and supportive throughout the process of putting together this book, and I'm lucky to have had your insights and passion for history and writing on my side. And to Zoe Ames, my copyeditor, thank you for your talent and attention to detail. Your honest, insightful feedback has undoubtedly made this book much more valuable to me and the people reading this.

To Shaun Curtis and Sarah Hedlund, huge thanks to both of you for advising me on how to structure this book. Shaun, I remember reading your book *Gaithersburg: Then & Now* several times over when I was a kid, and now your local expertise has informed two of my own books. Sarah, you have been so helpful and gracious, both in my family history efforts and in helping pick out the photos and topics to cover out of countless choices for my work.

To the people who have helped my writing grow and mature over the years, thank you for inspiring me to create and polish and practice and keep getting better. To list a few, thank you to Ira Chinoy, Michael Olmert and Evva Starr. I didn't come out of college with an English or journalism degree, but I will have a lifelong passion for writing and fact-finding fueled by the skills you have taught me.

While researching for and writing this book, I've met so many wonderful personalities who have generously shared their stories with me. You all have worked alongside me to make sure I get the facts right and to get the most crucial ones; I'm blown away by how many people have been so willing to help. Thank you to the following people, who have contributed their time, information and/or photos to this project: Joe Acanfora, Shirley Appleby, Merhlyn Barnes, Joanne Barnhart, Bernardine Beall, Chris Berger, Matt Blazi, Megan Boblitt, Susan Boblitt, Robert Booher, Carrie Boyd, Hallie Butler-Van Horn and the Butler family, Robert Chiswell, Lynne Chiswell, Brian Crane, Laine Crosby, Kevin Davey, Courtney Davis, Kisha Davis, Kenneth Day, Jennifer Boresz Engelking, Warren Fleming, Frances Foreman, Jeanne Gartner, Ida Pearl Green, Rita Green, Lisa Guidry-Moore, Justin Harclerode, Meredith Horan, Betty Huber, Lee Huber, Jean Hulse-Hayman, Derek Jackson, Terry LaMotte, Kathy Lehman, Karen Yaffe Lottes, Julianne Mangin, Jerry McCoy, Amanda McCurry, Forrest Milner, Frances Mills, Mark Mills, Corlin Moore, Daniel Myrick, Patricia Patula, Marilynn Randall, Eduardo Sánchez, Ben Snouffer, Diana Snouffer, Susan Cooke Soderberg, Maya Thompson, Glenn Wallace, Julia Wieseckel, Paul Wilson and Joann Snowden Woodson.

To the people who lift me up every day and have gotten even more excited about this book than I have, I'm blessed to have you in my life, and I sincerely thank you. That includes my parents, Carol and Greg Myers; my siblings, Amanda and Mike Myers; my grandmother Grace Walker; as well as Chase Blum, Jacob Toll, JT Woods, Corinne Wright and many others. It's easy to appreciate the lives of others when you all constantly help me to appreciate mine.

# PART I

# EARLY MoCo HISTORY

Chapter 1

# A Crash Course in Pre-MoCo History

O nce upon a time, a bunch of us watched the Disney movie *Pocahontas*, in which the title character, a member of the Powhatan tribe, falls in love with an English settler named Captain John Smith. While he may never have shared a voice with Mel Gibson, did you know that Captain Smith was likely the first White man to walk on Montgomery County soil?

In *real* life, Captain Smith was an early explorer of the Chesapeake Bay and the Potomac River, most likely traveling up as far as Great Falls for exploration in 1608. He was perhaps the first White man to ever come across tribes like the Piscataways and Anacostans, who evidently found great success hunting and fishing in the area. Fur trader Henry Fleet, who came to Great Falls in 1624, wrote, "The Indians in one night commonly will catch thirty sturgeons in a place where the river is not over twelve fathoms broad." He also remarked that the area was full of deer, bear, turkey and buffalo for them to hunt.

Yes, we apparently had bison in Montgomery County four hundred years ago! They were practically wiped out on the East Coast by the era of the American Revolution, but it's a fun piece of trivia nonetheless. Back in the seventeenth century, Native American tribes used bows and arrows, and sometimes rifles, to hunt animals like the buffalo. While they prospered at gaining sustenance for themselves, the tribes who lived in what is now our county struggled with diseases like consumption, pleurisy and smallpox. How did they try to get healthy again? With a hot oven and a cool river.

According to T.H.S. Boyd's *The History of Montgomery County*, the Natives believed that their panacea was simply to sweat out any illness, whether mild or severe. First, the afflicted person would crawl naked inside an earthen oven, heated with hot stones, until they felt a "profuse perspiration." Once the heat became too much, the patient would creep out of the oven and immediately charge into the Potomac or some other cold body of water. After about thirty seconds in the water, they would repeat this process for a second and third time before finally smoking a pipe "with composure." Boyd notes that "in many cases a cure was completely effected."

Although adventurers like Smith and Fleet visited the area of present-day Montgomery County early in the seventeenth century, Maryland's proprietary government did not start offering land grants in the area until 1688. In 1696, this land finally became part of a county, Prince George's County, established eighty years before Montgomery County. Imagine: if this were still the case, MoCo residents could say they live in the same county as the University of Maryland, Six Flags America and multiple Bojangles franchises.

Dowden's Ordinary, once located in Clarksburg. *Library of Congress (hereafter LOC).*

At separate times, Founding Father Benjamin Franklin (*left*) and General Edward Braddock (*right*) attempted to stay at Dowden's Ordinary. Portrait by Frederick James, circa 1906. *LOC.*

Economically, we were doing all right for ourselves back when we were in P.G. County. We didn't have the best soil in our area—rockier and rougher than the farmland closer to the Chesapeake—but "pre-MoCo" still managed to have great success selling Maryland's signature cash crop, tobacco. During the eighteenth century, close to 20 percent of Maryland's tobacco exports came from the farms in present-day Montgomery County. One of these historic farms, Prospect Hill, was built in 1724, and its farmhouse built in 1783 still stands on the property near Brookeville.

The tobacco industry had a great social impact on Central Maryland as well. Planters in the northern reaches of the county needed to transport their goods dozens of miles south to the commercial center of Georgetown (once part of Maryland, now Washington, D.C.). As they commuted across some of the area's earliest roads, inns and taverns began to pop up to offer travelers a place to rest and refuel on their journeys. Two of Montgomery County's first towns, Rockville and Clarksburg, began to form in the 1750s with the rise of Owen's Ordinary and Dowden's Ordinary, respectively. The term *ordinary* referred to a tavern or inn during this time.

In 1748, the county we know and love today gained another new identity, Frederick County, after the Maryland General Assembly created the county from parts of Baltimore and Prince George's Counties. While they lived in Frederick County, residents of the Clarksburg area may have gotten to meet figures like President George Washington, General Edward Braddock and Benjamin Franklin. In her article "History of Clarksburg—2015," the Clarksburg Historical Society's Jean Hulse-Hayman writes that General Braddock and his aide, a young Washington, stayed at Dowden's Ordinary for a night in 1755 during the French and Indian War. The following

*The Death of General Montgomery in the Attack on Quebec, December 31, 1775,* by John Trumbull, 1786. *LOC.*

day, General Braddock and Washington continued their march north toward Fort Duquesne, Pennsylvania. While Washington would survive the expedition—and many more conflicts—Braddock would die later that year in the Battle of the Monongahela.

Hulse-Hayman also acknowledges that Ben Franklin intended to stay the night at Dowden's Ordinary. However, Franklin found that the inn was full, so he ended up staying with a local farmer instead. To top it all off, one local rumor says that President Andrew Jackson ate dinner here on the way to his inauguration in 1829.

By the 1770s, Owen's Ordinary in Rockville had become Hungerford's Tavern—and would become a historical landmark in its own right. On June 16, 1774, the *Maryland Gazette* published five resolutions from "a meeting of a respectable and numerous body of the freemen of the lower part of Frederick county, at Charles Hungerford's tavern, on Saturday eleventh day of June, 1774." These resolutions protested the excessive taxation by the British of the colonists, expressed support of the recent Boston Tea Party and announced the body's intention to send ten of its members as representatives to a meeting of the Maryland General Assembly. You might recognize two of the ten Patriots listed, "Doctor Thomas Sprigg Wootton" and "Zadok Magruder." It looks like these local high school namesakes were drinking buddies back in the day.

Dr. Wootton also felt that it would be easier for residents of Frederick County if they did not have to travel so far to reach their seat of government, then in the town of Frederick. If you lived in what is now Bethesda, for instance, you would have to travel more than thirty miles to reach the courthouse. Yes, you wouldn't have to deal with the traffic on I-270, but you also wouldn't have a car or a modern highway system. Thus, in summer 1776, Wootton proposed during the final session of Maryland's Annapolis Convention to divide Frederick County into three counties to create two new counties. One would be named Washington County in honor of George Washington, who at the time was commanding the Continental army in the American Revolution. The other new county would be named Montgomery County, in honor of General Richard Montgomery, even though he likely never stepped foot here. General Montgomery had died six months earlier while fighting British forces. Montgomery led his men into Canada to try to gain the French Canadians as allies for the Americans, but the campaign failed, and Montgomery was killed at the Battle of Quebec on New Year's Eve 1775. Like Wootton and Magruder, Montgomery would also get a local high school named in his honor.

On September 6, 1776, the Annapolis Convention passed Wootton's bill into law, and Montgomery County, Maryland, was born. No more worrying about having to go to court all the way in Frederick. So where was the most appropriate place for the new county seat? The founding fathers of Montgomery County already knew what a great meeting spot they had in Hungerford's Tavern. The votes came in, and Hungerford's Tavern became the first courthouse ever for Montgomery County, Maryland. The community of Rockville sprouted around it and became the county seat we have today.

## Chapter 2

# GEORGETOWN COLLEGE, BUT LATER UNIVERSITY, OF MARYLAND, BUT EVEN LATER OF WASHINGTON, THE DISTRICT OF COLUMBIA

I wonder if the students from Maryland who go to Georgetown University ever wish that they lived in alternate universe. Could there be an alternate universe where they could get public, in-state tuition?

A long, long time ago, Georgetown was still private, but there were two years in history where Maryland students could, hypothetically, have been considered in-state. When it was established in 1789 as Georgetown College, the school lay within the bounds of Georgetown, *Maryland*, Montgomery County's only town at the time.

Georgetown was established in 1751 on the Potomac River, rapidly becoming a vital port of trade with places like Glasgow, Scotland. When the tobacco trade in Southern Maryland dried up, businessmen came north to the Georgetown area for better trading opportunities. Farmers from across Montgomery County would bring their tobacco and wheat to Georgetown, where it would be inspected, stored and then shipped across the Atlantic Ocean. For years, the humble town of Georgetown even rivaled established tobacco markets like Alexandria and Baltimore. As noted in *A Grateful Remembrance* by Richard K. MacMaster and Ray Eldon Hiebert, Maryland's first governor, Thomas Johnson, admired the port town for its impressive operations as a market for Montgomery County's high-quality tobacco. In a 1791 letter to George Washington, he wrote:

> *George Town, a good port for shipping in this county, has for some years past been the best market for tobacco in the state, perhaps in America.*

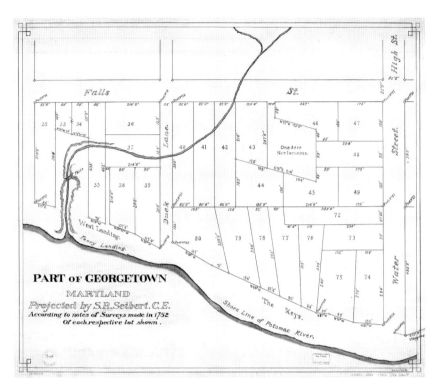

A map of Georgetown based on its layout in 1752. This map reflects the time in history when Georgetown was a part of Maryland. *LOC.*

Sketch of Georgetown College, published by Casimir Bohn, circa 1800. *LOC.*

While Roman Catholic bishop John Carroll established what was then Georgetown College in 1789, students would not start matriculating there until 1792. In this short span of time, something big happened. In 1791, George Washington picked out the general area of Washington, D.C., as the location for the new capital of the United States. This resulted in the towns of Alexandria and Georgetown becoming parts of the new federal city, leaving Maryland and Virginia with less land.

Although Congress would retrocede Alexandria back to Virginia in 1846, Georgetown has remained separate from Maryland for over two hundred years. Talks have persisted over the years about whether Georgetown should rejoin Montgomery County, Maryland, leading to a greater political question: should Washington, D.C., gain statehood by being absorbed into Maryland? Only time will tell whether one day Georgetown will return to MoCo like a prodigal son and Marylanders at Georgetown University may come one step closer to getting in-state tuition.

## Chapter 3

# WOODSTOCK

## *George Washington's Farm That Time Once Forgot*

Driving down Route 28 past Darnestown and Beallsville, almost into Dickerson, you'll pass by an inconspicuous marker indicating an astounding piece of history. Blink and you'll miss the sign that says the property shrouded in trees to your right was once owned by the first president of the United States. Today, historians believe it is George Washington's last surviving tenant house on the Woodstock farm.

Not much has been recorded about the history of Woodstock. Historians had previously been misled by the fact that Thomas Peter, the man who took ownership of Woodstock after Washington, also owned land near Seneca called Montevideo. Thomas Peter was the husband of George Washington's step-granddaughter, Martha Parke Custis Peter. The Peter family would go on to use Montevideo as a summer residence.

In the early 1950s, a historian from Takoma Park named Olive Hoover got a strange feeling on learning more about the Montevideo property. Hoover noticed that Washington's schedule of property from July 1799 states that the farm owned by Washington was located "about 30 miles above the city of Washington, not far from Kittoctan." Montevideo is only about twenty-one miles from downtown Washington, D.C., as the crow flies, while Woodstock is about thirty miles away using the same method. Katherine Scarborough's 1953 *Baltimore Sun* article "George Washington's Maryland Farms" goes into detail about how Hoover teamed up with fellow historian Roger Brooke Farquhar and land patent expert Dr. Arthur G. Tracey to research and finally point out the real location of Washington's farm at Woodstock.

"Montevideo" house, near Seneca, photographed by John O. Brostrup, 1936. This farm was mistaken for the site of George Washington's tenant house until the early 1950s. *LOC.*

Hoover's research ultimately shed light on the true location as well as the history of Washington's property in Montgomery County. What we now know is that the property was established in 1725 as 1,102 acres by Thomas Sprigg Jr. His granddaughter Sophia Sprigg married John Francis Mercer, who served as the tenth governor of Maryland from 1801 to 1803. While marrying into the Mercer family gave her a certain political prestige, Sophia lost almost half of her grandfather's property because of her marriage. Her father-in-law had owed a debt to Washington, so to finally pay him back, Mercer took 519 acres of his wife's land and ceded it to Washington in 1794.

Mary-Margaret Boblitt currently lives on the farm with her husband, Michael Palaszynski. Her parents, Susan and Michael, have visited over the years to lend their help with preserving the property. Since Boblitt acquired the property in 2011, her family has done extensive research on their historic home. "We have 6.8 acres zoned with the house. We're on the only historical part of the parcel left, and we have the only one of Washington's three tenant houses here left," Boblitt said.

Washington never lived at Woodstock, but from 1794 to his death in 1799, he allowed tenants to live on his farm in exchange for the crops they grew there. Evidently, this was not a fun experience for Washington, since his letters around this time mention how his tenants struggled to pay rent and the tobacco crop did not flourish there. One tenant named Priscilla Beale wrote to Washington pleading for leniency after his rent collector came and she couldn't afford to pay him. She explained that her family was sick with consumption (tuberculosis), the market for the wheat she had grown was unfavorable and she couldn't sustain the growth of tobacco there. "G.W. was not a great farmer; he was more experimental," Boblitt's mother, Susan, added. "Tobacco just wouldn't grow here; they probably grew rye or oats, wheat and small Indian corn."

The history of the property between the 1800s and the early 1950s is somewhat blurry since not much documentation appears to exist. The Boblitts have gotten clues about the property from the physical hints in and around their house. Along the creek next to Woodstock, treasure hunters with metal detectors have found old spent bullets, buckles and buttons from the Civil War. Back then, did soldiers use Woodstock as a makeshift hospital?

Under the front stairs of the house, a signature on the wood reads, in penciled cursive, "Built by W.T. Hilton, Jun. 29, 1899." A native of nearby Barnesville, William T. Hilton was a prominent builder of private homes in Montgomery County as well as an undertaker. In 1890, he founded Hilton Funeral Home, now a sixth-generation family business and one of the most well-known funeral homes in Montgomery County. Hilton's signature would indicate that the newer front half of the house was built in 1899.

The Boblitts have determined that the back half of the house and the property's corncrib most likely date to pre-1800. Handmade rosehead nails line the corncrib, while logs made of now-extinct white chestnut line the exterior of the older half of the house. The home's mortise and tenon joints are characteristic of a project constructed prior to the nineteenth century, as land records suggest this one was.

Other features of Woodstock include a root cellar, a grain barn and, curiously enough, old baby clothes. When the Boblitts moved in, they were shocked to discover an old box of nineteenth-century infant gowns with notes written from that era by the family of Betsey Otis Perkins. Five of Betsey's children wore one of the gowns, while a grandchild named Robert Perkins Evans wore another. The author of one of the notes identified herself as one of Robert's sisters and wrote that Robert died in 1859 at three years old. What's even weirder is that on further research, I found that Betsey's family had no clear connection to the farm. In fact, they lived in New London, Connecticut, and Buda, Illinois, nowhere near MoCo. Could Woodstock have been their summer home? Or could a previous resident have purchased these artifacts from an antique shop, leaving the treasures behind for the Boblitts to find?

In 2011, a twenty-five-year-old Boblitt made a decision she says took a lot of "chutzpah" and bought the Woodstock property. Back then, she claims, it was a decision made out of her "toxic relationship with old houses." The property was close to her work and family, right down the street from Woodstock Equestrian Park and had low interest rates as part of the

The Boblitts' home at Woodstock. The left side shows the part of the house added in 1899, while the right side dates to before 1800. *Author's collection.*

Montgomery County Agricultural Reserve. Her heart sank when she fully realized the state of the house. "I didn't move in right away, it was unlivable, moldy…carpet full of stinkbugs, crunchy…biblical level of insects there," Boblitt said. "Eventually, I lived in a tent in the living room. I was woken up twice by a giant toad, but to be fair, there were probably more bugs to eat inside than outside."

It had only been two years since the last owners moved out, but the house was already showing signs of distress. The house had changed hands many times from the 1950s to 2011, and keeping up the old property was a constant challenge. The owners just before Boblitt had spent a lot of time and money restoring Woodstock and were featured in an early 2000s episode of HGTV's *Old Homes Restored*. Ultimately, Boblitt made it her mission to preserve the property. "Burst water pipes, broken windows and a resident black snake or two. There were infestations of squirrels and North American roof rats to take care of and a lot of heavy lifting required," Boblitt said. "It's cost $50,000 to $60,000 just to preserve the logs from time and termites. Every year, they get treated. We had the logs cleaned and put a gentle satin finish over to preserve them."

The road to recovery hasn't been easy for Woodstock, but thanks to the Boblitt family, this historical masterpiece is again getting the care it deserves. Mary-Margaret loves her "Franken-house," a home full of influences ranging from the days of Washington the landlord until now.

Yes, it's full of different influences from different time periods—oh, and possibly ghosts. Stick around for that chapter.

Chapter 4

# First There's the Poorhouse,
# Then There's Prison

W hen I was on the Wootton High School track team, my favorite days were the days we got to go on road runs. During these practices, the team would run up and down Wootton Parkway, watching cars pass and messing around as we caught up on each other's school day and, on some days, passing by the Montgomery County Detention Center. "Coach'll throw you in there if you don't pick up the pace," I remember one guy saying to another.

It wasn't that long ago that the prison we joked about getting sent to was the poorhouse everyone wanted to avoid. Before it was the detention center, the Montgomery County Poor Farm housed mentally challenged, disabled and poor folks in the area for 170 years. It opened in 1789 and began by serving as both a poorhouse and a workhouse.

According to a 1998 article by Patricia Abelard Andersen for the Montgomery County Historical Society, anyone received into the almshouse had to wear a badge on the right shoulder of their outermost clothing. The badge read "PM," as in "poor" and "Montgomery." If any new resident refused to take on the badge, they would take no more than fifteen lashings instead. If a resident sent to the workhouse acted disorderly or refused to work, this would also lead to fifteen lashings.

Given its setting reminiscent of *One Flew Over the Cuckoo's Nest*, it is not surprising that the poor farm has had a controversial history. In 1877, the county commissioned an investigation of the conditions of the property, which highlighted the racial disparities between how White

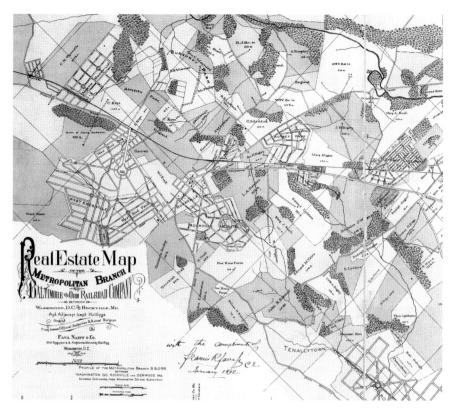

A map of the Baltimore & Ohio Railway in 1890. The poor farm is marked right below "Rockville Heights" on the map. *LOC.*

and Black residents were treated at the facilities. While the ten White inmates had spacious and comfortable rooms, the eighteen Black inmates found themselves much more cramped. In reference to the Black male inmates, the report stated, "The sleeping apartment for the ten males is ten by twelve feet only, with one window, their sitting room is entirely too small." Meanwhile, the farm and outbuildings were marked as being in good condition.

In 1901, the county reported finding twenty-seven inmates at the poor farm, thirteen White and fourteen Black. This update stated, "Everything was most gratifying to the visiting committee and in most excellent condition." Yet just six years later, readers of the *Sunday Star* would wake up to see the following headline splashed across the front page of the Special Features section: "Almshouse conditions disgraceful, declares Montgomery Grand Jury."

This December 1907 report demonstrates how atrocious the conditions of the poor farm had gotten by the early 1900s. The grand jury discussed how the main building had plaster that was falling apart; exposed, rusty nails; and a porch that was rotting to collapse. The outhouses for the inmates, many of whom were old and disabled, were about fifty to one hundred yards away from their buildings, and many of these inmates weren't physically able to reach them on their own. The article repeatedly mentions an "idiotic janitor" whose job was to clean the outhouses even though many weaker inmates could not reach them. Since the bathing area was also not easily reachable, this meant that many inmates also went without bathing themselves regularly.

One man, who lived in the "colored" section of the house, was reportedly crippled and terminally ill. He had used the same chair for the past fifty years and would refuse to leave his room to clean himself, wearing five shirts at a time when the older ones became "soiled." According to the grand jury that visited him, the smell in his room was "unbearable."

The revelations of the 1907 report acted as a wake-up call for the local community. Over the next several years, women's organizations such as the Montgomery County Social Service League and the Woman's Christian Temperance Union worked together to appropriate money for the repairs that the facilities, now called the County Home, desperately needed. Social workers and the American Red Cross stepped in to help the home's residents, young and old, by providing sewing lessons, a new piano and necessities like wheelchairs.

The women of Montgomery County performed remarkably to improve the welfare of residents at the County Home. Just sixteen years after one Washington news article remarked that inmates couldn't move from their bedrooms to the bathroom, the *Washington Times* reported that they took a trip to the circus in 1923. A Miss Naomi Bogley and County Commissioner Lacey Shaw organized the trip, taking all the residents to Washington for the show, followed by a dinner downtown for everyone prepared by Commissioner Shaw's sister-in-law. From 1921 to 1923, the conditions at the County Home drastically improved. What was once a shame to the community had become, according to one 1923 *Times* article, an institution of "first-class condition."

As the Great Depression rolled in with the 1930s, President Franklin D. Roosevelt offered a slew of New Deal programs that would greatly affect the fate of the County Home. In 1935, he passed the Social Security Act, providing financial assistance to the elderly and establishing a program for

The Rockville Poor Farm, also known as the Alms House, prior to being torn down in 1959. Today, a detention center stands in its place. *Montgomery County Historical Society (hereafter MCHS), photographed by Lewis Reed.*

unemployment insurance. What with these new benefits and the increasing popularity of private nursing homes, the almshouse became a burden for the local government to run. Eventually, the property was abandoned.

In 1957, construction of US Route 240 (now I-270) led to the destruction of the farm on the County Home's property, and in 1959, the almshouse was torn down to make way for the new Montgomery County Detention Center. The poor farm cemetery on Rockville's Monroe Street, full of hundreds of unmarked graves, stands as a lone, humble reminder of the lives left to ebb away there. We can only imagine what could have led them here.

We don't know too much about the inmates who went to live at the Montgomery County Poor Farm. These people, labeled "aged," "deaf and dumb" and "idiotic," were trapped in a time and place that didn't cater to mental and physical disabilities as well as modern institutions like Shady Grove or Suburban Hospital do. One thing can be said about this property: it is a prison now, just like it was a prison then.

Chapter 5

# The Lost Town of Triadelphia

A long the northeastern border of Montgomery County, a large reservoir on the Patuxent River breaks up Montgomery and Howard Counties from each other. The reservoir draws fishermen for its stockage of sunfish, catfish and walleye. Families come to the reservoir for its playgrounds and scenic hiking trails along the water. Kayaking, barbecuing, picnicking: it's no wonder so many people come here every summer.

When the reservoir was built in 1943, it was given the name Triadelphia Lake. Why? Before there was the lake, there was Triadelphia, a once bustling town whose remnants lie at the bottom of the reservoir like the lost city of Atlantis. Underneath the bass boats and blue water, there once was a town where hundreds of people lived throughout much of the nineteenth century.

In 1809, founders Thomas Moore, Caleb Bentley and Isaac Briggs needed a name for the new town they were establishing and decided to choose one that celebrated the familial bond they shared. Each of the men married one of the daughters of Roger and Mary Brooke, the family namesake for the nearby town of Brookeville. Since these unions made the three men brothers-in-law, they called their new town Triadelphia, a Greek word which loosely translates to "three brothers" in English.

All three men were accomplished professionals in their own right. Moore patented an early version of the refrigerator, Bentley was the first postmaster of Brookeville and Briggs was one of the chief engineers in the construction of the Erie Canal. They began building up Triadelphia with a cotton mill, followed by a gristmill, sawmill and several houses where the workers would live.

The War of 1812 offered great business opportunities for the men as more and more Americans refused to buy any products from Britain, eliminating competition for Triadelphia's mills. Men, women and children worked in the factory as the town's population grew to more than three hundred. On May 16, 1812, Briggs wrote to his dear friend, President James Madison, about the recent success of American industry. He asked the president if he might send the postmasters to collect data on how mill production had increased across the country, to encourage millworkers to keep up the good work. About Triadelphia, he mentioned: "P.S. I have been about 20 months engaged in spinning cotton. The experiment is encouraging."

After the war ended, milling in Triadelphia took a turn for the worse. In the colder, drier climate of Maryland, cotton could not be grown and had to be shipped into the Port of Baltimore. This was one cost for the Maryland cotton mills, but Triadelphia was at even more of a disadvantage being in rural Montgomery County, dozens of miles from Baltimore and only accessible by poorly maintained country roads. The cost of transport from the South to Baltimore and then from Baltimore to Triadelphia forced them to raise the minimum selling price for their cotton. Competing mills closer to the Port of Baltimore with greater access to resources like spindles and labor kept Triadelphia from attracting more business to the town. A recession in the late 1810s also set the factory up for disaster.

After the deaths of Briggs and Moore and the financial downfall of the mill, Bentley had had enough of the Triadelphia cotton business. In 1830, sixty-eight-year-old Bentley, Moore's descendants and another partner named Bernard Gilpin sold the factory to Bernard's son, Samuel Gilpin. Gilpin, now saddled with massive amounts of debt, abandoned the venture after six years, and his successor, Edward Painter, only lasted four.

While the two previous owners may have been scarred by their experiences at Triadelphia, Thomas Lansdale at least had a love-hate relationship with the property. He bought the mill at Triadelphia in 1840, and although he left it for eleven years to operate another mill closer to Baltimore, he managed Triadelphia for twenty-seven years, and it remained in his family until 1923. Lansdale faced many hardships throughout his time at Triadelphia and never restored it to its former glory, but he helped the population reach four hundred and he kept business there going until his death in 1878. Locals knew and respected Lansdale as the owner of the mill and as a Maryland state senator in the mid-1860s.

If there were ever a fixer-upper of a town in the nineteenth century, Triadelphia was it. First, a fire in 1843 burned down the entire mill and caused $25,000 in damages, equivalent to over $1,000,000 in today's dollars. Then, in 1860, another fire destroyed not only several mill buildings but Lansdale's house too, leaving him; his wife, Harriet; and their six children homeless. The beginning of the Civil War also meant that southern Confederate states weren't providing cotton to the North anymore, causing the mill to shut down indefinitely.

Still, the townspeople evidently had pride in their community. According to an 1860 report from Triadelphia in the *Baltimore Sun*, "Thrift and activity are apparent in the neighborhood at this time." The representative also boasted that the town produced "the well-known brand of Triadelphia 4-4 brown muslin" and that in the past several weeks, "some forty persons have professed conversion [to Methodism], a number of whom are heads of families."

The resilience of the community helped them battle through their hardships, but misfortune ran them out of town in the end. In 1868, operators had decided to work on restarting the cotton mill when the Patuxent River overflowed its banks, causing a massive flood to wash out much of the town. The gristmills remained, but after almost sixty years, cotton production in Triadelphia had come to an end.

Then came May 31, 1889. Massive rainstorms, a faulty dam and subsequent flooding killed 2,208 people in Johnstown, Pennsylvania. Less than two hundred miles away, rain poured heavily onto Triadelphia and the Patuxent River, creating a flood that would lead to loss not of lives but of livelihood. The week after the tragedy, the *Montgomery County Sentinel* reported, "Thomas Lansdale's mill, at Triadelphia, received damage that amounts to a wreck and his house was flooded, his family wading in water waist deep to make their escape from it." With their homes and workplaces destroyed, residents left in droves to try to rebuild what they had lost in the flood somewhere else.

After this flood, the town quickly became what many called a "deserted village." Just as quickly as people had come, most of them had left. The town continued to deteriorate over the next fifty years, until just two families lived there. Fewer and fewer people lived in Triadelphia during the twentieth century, but more and more people began to visit the town for recreational purposes. The riverside ruins offered a great spot for swimming, camping and picnicking at the Patuxent.

The Washington Suburban Sanitary Commission (WSSC) was eyeing Triadelphia for different reasons. The commission's chief engineer, Harry R. Hall, worried that due to the rapid growth of cities like Arlington, Virginia,

Triadelphia Mill, as captured in 1936 by Delos H. Smith. *LOC.*

Montgomery and Prince George's Counties would not be able to rely on the water supply provided by Washington, D.C. In 1941, he led the WSSC's efforts to build a dam and reservoir at Triadelphia, which would provide a more abundant water supply for cities like Rockville and Bowie.

The following year, the WSSC acquired what remained of Triadelphia, evicted the few residents who still lived there and knocked down what buildings were left. The WSSC flooded Triadelphia one more time, finally washing it out for good, and in 1943, Triadelphia Lake and the Brighton Dam were completed.

Today, a few traces of the old town survive. A small cemetery is one of them, and another is the "Triadelphia Bell," a bell made in 1837 and rung to let the town know that the workday had begun. In 1902, the bell was transferred to the nearby Sherwood Academy in Sandy Spring to signal the start of the school day. The bell remains there—only now, Sherwood Academy is Sherwood High School.

As Montgomery County grew into the metropolitan area it is today, what was once one of its most successful towns lies silent at the bottom of a fishing lake. Even in silence, the past has a way of making an appearance. A sediment removal project in 2023 required the WSSC to partially drain the lake, turning up old stone foundations and making curious observers wonder: What was going on down there?

Chapter 6

# A Bloody Battle, $3,000 Skirts and Other Tales from the Civil War

I t didn't get much more borderline than Montgomery County. It was split between Union and Confederate loyalties, and close to one third of the county's citizens owned slaves. The following stories took place during the 1860s, when the county served as a critical passage between the North and the South.

During the Civil War, liquor became a necessary evil as soldiers battled homesickness and shell shock from their time in service. On October 18, 1861, the *Montgomery County Sentinel* reported on the tragedy that occurred at Darnestown eleven days earlier, while the Fifth Connecticut Infantry was setting up camp and making dinner during a severe storm.

In the midst of the chaos, a man started distributing liquor that he had smuggled into camp, and some of the soldiers became intoxicated. By the time the officers noticed, it was too late. A drunken fight ensued that left one man dead, a few others wounded and several cattle and horses shot. Following this event, the officers made more of an effort to punish offenders caught with alcohol or found to be intoxicated and destroy any traces of what the *Sentinel* called a "villainous beverage."

On October 21, 1861, the Battle of Ball's Bluff took place in Virginia across from Edwards Ferry, an important crossing point throughout the war. Heritage Montgomery's Life in a War Zone project comments that Ball's Bluff was notable for being the only instance in the Civil War when a U.S. senator was killed in action. Men were captured, shot or drowned while fighting along the Potomac River. Oregon senator and colonel Edward D.

Baker was mortally shot; his funeral services were held in Poolesville. Future Supreme Court justice Oliver Wendell Holmes was critically wounded during the battle but survived. The Confederates won this battle, but the war continued to rage.

Up north, Barnesville would suffer a severe identity crisis. The town changed hands five times on September 9, 1862, starting out as Confederate-occupied and ending up as Union-occupied by the end of the day. The residents of Barnesville saw troops that day marching up to the notorious Battle of Antietam. In late June 1863, they would see more marching through their town up to Gettysburg.

Rockville was a hot spot for Confederate activity, and Unionist Dora Higgins found herself at the center of it. On June 28, 1863, as she prepared her children for Sunday school, she realized that Confederate troops were closing in on the town. She ran to Christ Episcopal Church to warn her husband, John, and other churchgoers to hide. When she returned to the family store, she found Confederate general J.E.B. Stuart's men at her front door, demanding that she unlock it for them. Her subsequent refusal

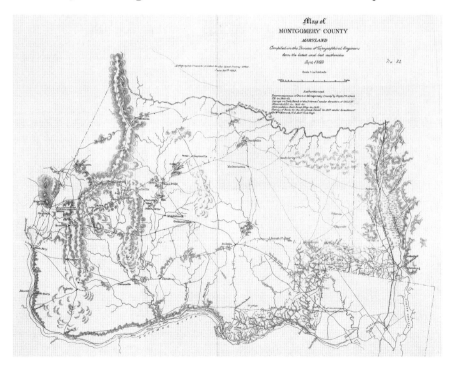

Map of Montgomery County, Maryland, in 1862. Around this time, Olney was known as Mechanicsville, Wheaton as Leesborough and Potomac as Offutt's Crossroads. *LOC.*

The old DeSellum house, Summit Hall, in Gaithersburg before it was remodeled. *MCHS.*

apparently impressed General Stuart, who ordered her to "let one of [his men] dare resist you."

For six hours, Dora held out against the "Rebels," before they finally left after looting supplies from other parts of town. John Higgins was found that evening hiding in the church and arrested by the men for his ties to the Union. He returned several hours later, having been released closer to Laytonsville because keeping John and the rest of their prisoners would have slowed down the soldiers' march toward Gettysburg. According to letters Dora wrote to her mother, Stuart's men would release hundreds more in Brookeville and Claggettsville. Looking back on the event, Dora wrote to her mother about how the Confederates behaved better than she expected, even though, she claimed, "they were going to run all the Yankees off the face of the Earth." She recalled one of them saying, "But we are gentlemen. We don't distress women and children and we don't destroy dwellings."

Thanks to Dora's warning, John DeSellum left Rockville immediately and escaped capture. In July 1864, Confederate general Jubal Early and his men raided DeSellum's home, Summit Hall, in Gaithersburg, taking all

*Right*: In 1863, Dora Higgins stood her ground against General J.E.B. Stuart and lived to tell the tale. Stuart was killed in battle the following year. *MCHS*.

*Below*: This photograph of Poolesville was taken in the winter of 1862. During this time, the Eighth Minnesota Infantry Regiment held it for the Union. *MCHS*.

The Union Arch Bridge at Cabin John, 1865. Completed in 1864, the bridge has faced controversy for its plaque honoring Confederate president Jefferson Davis. *LOC.*

DeSellum's livestock, crops and fences with them. He and his sister Sarah did manage to conceal $3,000 from Early's troops, which she hid under her skirts.

During Early's same campaign through Montgomery County, the Confederates burned down Falkland, the Silver Spring home of Postmaster General Montgomery Blair. Blair was a good friend of President Abraham Lincoln and had represented Dred Scott in the landmark 1857 case *Dred Scott v. Sandford*. Maryland's largest high school, located in Silver Spring, is named after him.

Five days after the end of the Civil War, on April 14, 1865, President Lincoln was assassinated. A manhunt began for the killer, John Wilkes Booth, and his coconspirators. One of the coconspirators, George Atzerodt, failed to fulfill his assignment to kill Vice President Andrew Johnson and fled to his cousin Hartman Richter's house in Germantown. Atzerodt was found there six days later and taken back to Washington, where he was hanged on July 7, 1865.

# PART II

# CHANGEMAKERS

## Chapter 7

# Josiah Henson, Passenger and Conductor on the Underground Railroad

The Underground Railroad was the figurative name for the network of land and sea routes that slaves took while attempting to escape to freedom. Many of them fled to safety above the Mason-Dixon line in the northern United States or Canada. Along the way, they would stop at safe houses and receive guidance and care from abolitionist allies. The abolitionists were brave men and women who could be fined or jailed if they were discovered helping runaways.

The Fugitive Slave Acts of 1793 and 1850 allowed masters to capture and return their slaves to the South. These laws pushed runaways farther into Canada, where they would be safe from the acts' implications. If a fugitive slave was captured, the punishment could consist of being sold to a different master or being whipped, beaten or even murdered. In Montgomery County, Maryland, figures like Josiah Henson took these risks to escape their lives as slaves.

Josiah Henson was born into slavery on June 15, 1789, in Charles County, Maryland. After trying to fight off an overseer from raping Henson's mother, Henson's father was punished by being sold to another master. Each remaining member of the family was later sold off at auction and separated from each other. In his 1876 autobiography, *Uncle Tom's Story of His Life: An Autobiography of the Rev. Josiah Henson*, he recalled his mother begging her new master, Isaac Riley, to buy Josiah as well.

> *She fell at his feet, and clung to his knees, entreating him in tones that a mother only could command, to buy her baby as well as herself, and spare to*

*her one, at least, of her little ones....As she crawled away from the brutal man, I heard her sob out, "Oh, Lord Jesus, how long, how long shall I suffer this way?"*

At around six years old, Henson went to live with Adam Robb, a tavernkeeper in Rockville. Young Henson suffered starvation and grave illness under Robb's ownership. Fearing the little boy might die, Robb sold him to Isaac Riley, where Henson reunited with his mother, his "best friend on earth," and recovered in her care.

In his autobiography, Henson recounts the story of how he once helped Riley defeat an adversary named Brice Letton during a tavern brawl. Hungry for revenge, Letton ambushed Henson one day the following week while the latter was working. Letton brutally broke and maimed Henson's arm. He then beat his back with a pipe, breaking both shoulder blades.

Despite his harsh environment, Henson grew up to be a strong, valuable worker for Isaac Riley, eventually becoming the head of operations on his farm in what is now North Bethesda. During the late 1820s, he went to Kentucky to help Riley with a work trip, and with permission, he was allowed to travel from town to town earning money by preaching. He struck up a deal with Riley to buy his freedom for $100, but Riley later cheated him out of the deal by adding an extra zero. Unable to afford a $1,000 deal and fearful that he might be sold again, Henson planned an escape.

On a dark night in September 1830, Henson; his wife, Charlotte; and their children began their dangerous journey north from Kentucky. A fellow slave risked his life to push their boat off so they could cross the Ohio River into Indiana. The family suffered exhaustion and hunger on their monthlong journey. At one point, Charlotte Henson became so weak that she fainted as she tried to climb over a log. Luckily, her family was able to revive her.

With the help of Good Samaritans, Josiah Henson and his family continued to make their way north. During their travels, they met a White woman who defied her husband's wishes and gave the starving family free food to sustain them on the way to Cincinnati. There was also a ship captain who ferried the family across Lake Erie from Ohio to Buffalo, New York. On the morning of October 28, 1830, the Hensons landed on the shores of Canada. Josiah rolled around ecstatically in the sand and got up to embrace his family.

Henson spent the rest of his life as a free Black man in Canada. There, he learned to read, purchased his own land and became an active preacher and mentor to the fugitive slaves who would join him. He returned to

MARIA WEEMS ESCAPING IN MALE ATTIRE

Anna Maria Weems in her disguise as a man, 1855. *From The Underground Railroad by William Still.*

Author and former slave Josiah Henson at eighty-seven years old in 1876. Harriet Beecher Stowe used Henson as the inspiration for the title character in her novel *Uncle Tom's Cabin. National Portrait Gallery, Smithsonian Institution.*

Kentucky, this time as a "conductor" on the Underground Railroad, leading slaves north to freedom. The first version of his autobiography, *The Life of Josiah Henson*, was published in 1849, when he was sixty years old.

Henson's narrative influenced author Harriet Beecher Stowe in creating the title character of her 1852 novel *Uncle Tom's Cabin.* Unfortunately, many Jim Crow–era theatrical adaptations of the novel diverted from Stowe's abolitionist message. They primarily cast White men in blackface and focused on perpetuating Black stereotypes.

Henson lived a long and active life, passing away in Dresden, Ontario, Canada, on May 5, 1883, one month before his ninety-fourth birthday. The house of Isaac Riley, once a master to Josiah Henson, is now known as Uncle Tom's Cabin and is located along Old Georgetown Road in North Bethesda.

Josiah Henson was not the only notable passenger or conductor on the Underground Railroad from Montgomery County. In 1841, he established the Dawn settlement for fugitive slaves wishing to settle freely in Canada. Enslaved members of the Weems family would come to settle there in the 1850s after their own escapes from Montgomery County. At about the age of fifteen, Anna Maria Weems escaped from slavery in Montgomery County, traveling north up to Dresden, Canada, disguised as a male carriage driver.

Prior to the end of the Civil War, the legal principle of *partus sequitur ventrem* dictated that any African American child would inherit the legal status of their mother. In the case of sisters Mary and Emily Edmonson from

*Left*: Abolitionist author Harriet Beecher Stowe; her father, Lyman Beecher; and her brother Henry Ward Beecher, circa 1861. *National Portrait Gallery, Smithsonian Institution.*

*Below*: An 1879 poster for a theatrical performance of *Uncle Tom's Cabin. LOC.*

the Sandy Spring area, their father was a free Black man, but their mother was enslaved, meaning they had to be slaves like their mother. In 1848, the Edmonson girls gained national attention for taking part in the largest nonviolent escape attempt on record. Mary, Emily and seventy-five other slaves were caught near Point Lookout, Maryland, hiding in boxes on the *Pearl* and trying to escape north via the Chesapeake Bay.

Fifteen-year-old Mary and thirteen-year-old Emily were shuffled from Washington, D.C., down to New Orleans and then back up to Alexandria, Virginia. Their father, Paul Edmonson, traveled to Brooklyn, New York, to plead for help from Harriet Beecher Stowe's brother, pastor and abolitionist Henry Ward Beecher. Beecher rallied the Plymouth Church congregation he led to raise the funds and successfully emancipate Mary and Emily.

After gaining their freedom, the sisters went up to New York to participate in antislavery rallies with abolitionist Frederick Douglass. Henry Beecher and his sister Harriet continued to support Mary and Emily by sending them to the Young Ladies' Preparatory School at Oberlin College. In 1853, the same year they arrived at Oberlin, Mary Edmonson died of tuberculosis and eighteen-year-old Emily returned to Washington to continue her schooling.

Emily Edmonson continued working as an abolitionist alongside her dear friend Frederick Douglass. She married Larkin Johnson and returned to Sandy Spring to start a family with him. In her later years, she lived in Anacostia, the same Washington neighborhood as Douglass. Edmonson died there in 1895 at the age of sixty.

The State of Maryland abolished slavery from its Constitution on November 1, 1864, finally giving tens of thousands of African Americans in Maryland their freedom. This result was a controversial one. Per Miranda Spivack's 2013 *Washington Post* article "The Not-Quite-Free State," 29,799 Marylanders (49.69 percent) voted to keep slavery and 30,174 (50.31 percent) voted to abolish it. Had just a few hundred more voters changed their mind and voted to keep slavery, enslaved Marylanders would have had to continue resorting to the use of the Underground Railroad.

Chapter 8

# DOCTOR BIRD

## *Sandy Spring's Most Beloved Deliveryman*

The story of Sandy Spring's Doctor Bird is one worthy of its own PBS period drama. A charismatic, passionate doctor arrives from the big city to a small town and changes the lives of its residents forever. He established a much-needed lifeline to MoCo with his founding of the Montgomery County General Hospital, an institution that still operates to this day.

Dr. Jacob Wheeler Bird Sr. was born on October 3, 1885, in the small community of West River in Anne Arundel County. His father was a farmer, while three of his mother's brothers were doctors, a career path he followed by pursuing an education at the University of Maryland School of Pharmacy. When he graduated from UMD in 1907, his yearbook listed his age, height and weight as twenty-one, 145 pounds and five feet, eleven inches, respectively. It also included his senior quote:

*What music surely can you find*
*As soft as voices which are kind?*

On graduating, Bird went to work at the University Hospital in Baltimore as an assistant surgeon. The following year, two wonderful things happened for him. First, he was promoted to assistant superintendent of the hospital, and then, one day, in walked nurse Mary Wilson. According to one *Baltimore Sun* article, Bird's coworkers noticed that from the first day Wilson appeared, Bird "formed a decided fondness for her." The article, published on September 8, 1910, revealed the couple's exciting news with the title "Physician and Nurse Wed: An Interesting Hospital Romance Reaches Culmination."

After finishing two years of residency at University Hospital, Bird felt called to serve a rural community with a severe need for better healthcare. In the summer of 1909, he moved into a house dozens of miles away in Sandy Spring. His wife resigned from the hospital not long after and came to live with her husband in their new home.

According to records from the Sandy Spring Museum, the town had six physicians when Bird came to town, but they were all older men who died within a decade of his arrival. Bird got into tackling his responsibilities as a physician right away. He tried to ensure that no patient would be left unattended for too long with a "blue flag" system, in which storekeepers flew blue flags from their businesses to signal to Bird whenever a person in town was sick. Bird's house was the primary spot where he provided his services during his early career.

In 1916, Bird decided that upper Montgomery County needed a hospital of its own. He started small, renting out a home called Wrenwood in the nearby community of Brinklow. In its first year of operations, Wrenwood Hospital had only five beds but managed to host sixty-four patients and perform forty-eight operations.

Like her husband, Mary Wilson Bird was becoming accomplished in her own right. While she raised the couple's three children, Helen, Wheeler and Jane, she became a fixture of the community. Her obituary in the *Montgomery County Sentinel* would state that Mrs. Bird actively involved herself in the Montgomery County chapter of the Red Cross. She also chaired the Maryland Council of Defense's committee on medicine and nursing and was the director of the Needlework Guild of America.

As both Jacob and Mary Bird were building immense success for themselves in Sandy Spring, tragedy struck their family in 1917. In November that year, an influenza epidemic struck the town, and Mary caught the illness. After five days of battling the virus, Mary Wilson Bird died on November 18, 1917. She was just thirty-three years old.

Mary's death left her husband a widower with three small children and a mission to better prepare his community for any future outbreaks. In 1918, he called a meeting with eighteen of the town's most reputable citizens to plead with them for their help in building a newer, better-equipped hospital. The audience was moved by his passion, and together, they donated enough money to immediately start work on the project. Over the next two years,

Bird and his community banded together to construct the Montgomery County General Hospital, a Sandy Spring institution that would serve the entire county. Wrenwood closed in 1919 as the new hospital prepared for a grand opening.

The construction project held out against three waves of the Spanish influenza epidemic over two years. When the fourth wave came along, Sandy Spring was hit hard, and although the hospital wasn't quite ready yet, Bird realized that his town desperately needed organized health care. Due to the emergency, Montgomery County General Hospital opened earlier than expected, in February 1920. The furniture had arrived, but the facilities still lacked much of the equipment and supplies needed. In the midst of a severe blizzard, an eight-member board of the hospital's Ladies Auxiliary sprang into action, providing linens, food and donations they had quickly gathered from across the county. Before the blizzard was over, the hospital's first five patients would be taken in and treated.

In his first year at Montgomery County General, Dr. Bird was joined by anesthetist Dr. Charles C. Tumbleson from Baltimore. Tumbleson specialized in medicine and pediatrics, relieving Bird of many of the

Dr. Jacob W. Bird, the founder of Montgomery General Hospital. *MCHS.*

Dr. Jacob W. Bird's house in Sandy Spring, photographed in 1999. The house is located on the aptly named Doctor Bird Road. *M-NCPPC.*

duties involved in administering care and treatment to patients. The two would work together on thirty years of procedures, including a surgery in November 1920 to attempt to save the life of bombing victim James Bolton, covered in a later chapter.

Even with another physician at the hospital, Bird couldn't slow down. He usually worked fourteen-hour days, with some allowances made for naps on a couch in his office, and according to his colleagues, he managed to stay chipper and look ten years younger than his true age despite the grueling work schedule. Bird was a general practitioner in the hospital, but his main specialties were delivering babies and performing surgeries.

Throughout the rest of his life, Dr. Bird worked for many social service and medical organizations within the state of Maryland. He dedicated his life to the community of Sandy Spring, once organizing a group to buy out a defunct bus service and restart it at a time when its citizens didn't have one. One year, when Sherwood High School didn't have enough money to hire an eleventh-grade teacher, Bird donated $900 to cover four years of a potential teacher's salary. In his fifties, he became a father again to two boys named Jimmy and Bill by his second wife, Jean Woolford Skinner, whom he married in 1935.

Dr. Jacob W. Bird poses with dozens of the children he delivered as babies, along with their mothers, in 1917. *Sandy Spring Museum.*

On July 1, 1959, about 1,500 people, including Maryland governor Millard Tawes, came together in Sandy Spring to celebrate the fiftieth anniversary of when Dr. Bird first came to town in a horse-drawn buggy. Tawes thanked him for building Montgomery County General and for his social and medical contributions to Montgomery County and the state of Maryland as a whole. Even President Dwight D. Eisenhower sent him a congratulatory telegram.

At the end of the ceremony, Bird was presented with a portrait painted in his honor and a new car to compensate for the thirty-five vehicles he had run through while making fifty years of house calls. Three months later, Dr. Bird and Jean Bird went down to Huntsville, Alabama, to visit his son Wheeler and Wheeler's wife, Doris. On October 25, 1959, the family was driving near Huntsville when another car ran a stop sign and broadsided them. Wheeler and Doris survived, but Dr. Bird and Jean were killed, just weeks after Bird's seventy-fourth birthday.

The tragedy sent shock waves through the community of Sandy Spring. They had lost one of their most beloved citizens in the very car they had given him. After his death, some locals tried unsuccessfully to change the name of Montgomery County General Hospital to "Dr. Jacob W. Bird

Memorial Hospital." While he was not able to be memorialized in this way, we now know the road where he lived and practiced on in Sandy Spring as Doctor Bird Road.

In over fifty years as a physician, Dr. Bird delivered over four thousand babies, once delivering five on his birthday. He never turned away a patient and worked effortlessly to secure a bright financial and medical future for Sandy Spring. From the time he started the hospital in 1920 to when he died in 1959, the number of beds increased from twenty-eight to seventy-two. Today, Montgomery County General Hospital is known as MedStar Montgomery Medical Center. It is one of eight hospitals in the county, has 138 beds and is one of only three county hospitals to have lasted more than one hundred years.

Chapter 9

# RACHEL CARSON'S *SILENT SPRING* FROM SILVER SPRING

Back in 1962, American conservationist Rachel Carson wrote *Silent Spring*, a groundbreaking book that exposed the dangers of pesticides, led to a ban on DDT and inspired the creation of the U.S. Environmental Protection Agency.

Rachel Carson moved into a new house in the Quaint Acres neighborhood of Silver Spring in 1957 under tragic circumstances. Her niece Marjorie had passed away, leaving a five-year-old son named Roger, so Carson stepped up and adopted the boy. She and Roger moved into a house Carson designed herself, built against the natural slope of the property so that the house would disturb its surroundings as little as possible. Wanting to make her property as green as she could, Carson planted several different types of flowers and trees around her house.

Carson was born in 1907 in Springdale, Pennsylvania, where she spent much of her early life. According to WETA journalist Patrick Kiger, Carson moved to Silver Spring to be close to her job with the Bureau of Fisheries (later the U.S. Fish and Wildlife Service). Prior to her move in 1957, she had lived in other Silver Spring homes, one on Flower Avenue and another on Williamsburg Drive. She also had lived in Baltimore and Takoma Park.

In the late 1950s, Carson became troubled by her research on a once-celebrated synthetic pesticide called DDT. DDT had been acclaimed for its effectiveness in killing insects and preventing the spread of diseases like typhus and malaria, as well as protecting crops from insects. Through her research, Carson realized that while DDT had some great benefits, it also came with

*Left*: Rachel Carson, 1944. *U.S. Fish and Wildlife Service.*

*Right*: The Rachel Carson House. *M-NCPPC.*

disastrous consequences. If a plant were sprayed with the substance, it could kill not only, for example, the locust on that plant but also any bird that ate or came into contact with the poisoned creature. DDT could affect humans, too, if the livestock we ate or drank milk from were tainted with it. As of 2023, the EPA acknowledges that both U.S. and international authorities classify DDT as a probable human carcinogen.

Carson spent four years of researching and writing from her house in Quaint Acres, and her *Silent Spring* was published in 1962. While the chemical industry tried to portray Carson as a lunatic, President John F. Kennedy and his administration backed the claims made in *Silent Spring* by leading their own research efforts to tackle the problem. The following decade, Carson's book helped to launch an Earth-conscious agenda for Americans. In 1970, we celebrated Earth Day for the first time and the EPA was launched. In 1972, DDT was officially banned by the EPA for its harmful effects on the environment.

Unfortunately, Carson never got to fully see the fruits of her labor. While trying to save those around her from a potential carcinogen, she herself was diagnosed with breast cancer. She died of the disease in 1964, only two years after the release of *Silent Spring*. She was buried at Rockville's Parklawn Memorial Park.

To date, *Silent Spring* has sold more than two million copies. In 1980, Carson posthumously received the Congressional Medal of Honor from President Jimmy Carter. In 1991, the house in Quaint Acres where she wrote the book was dedicated as a National Historic Landmark. Today, a 650-acre conservation park in Brookeville and an elementary school in Gaithersburg bear her name.

## Chapter 10

# GO WILDCATS!

## *The Story of Clarksburg's Wilson Wims*

What do you have to do to get an elementary school named after you? Let's look at the case of Wilson Wims. An outstanding figure in his hometown of Clarksburg and Montgomery County, Wims may be best remembered for providing Black workers affordable housing outside of Washington, D.C., and for leading the victorious Maryland Wildcats baseball team.

When Francis "Wilson" Wims was born in 1915, he became part of a family with deep roots in Montgomery County. As Ethel Gardiner Frye writes in *Wilson Wims: A Remarkable Life*, Wims's great-grandmother Martha Purdy Butler was "sold as a babe in arms along with her mother." After her release from slavery, Martha married George Butler and settled about a mile south of Hyattstown along what is now Route 355. In 1884, the Butlers gave land to build a new Methodist church called Montgomery Chapel for Hyattstown's Black community. Montgomery Chapel also served as a one-room schoolhouse for Black children, but it was frequently closed due to low enrollment, according to Mary Charlotte Crook of the Montgomery County Historical Society.

If you hike along Little Bennett Regional Park's Western Piedmont Trail, you'll come across a clearing called Wims Meadow. This was the "field of dreams" where Wilson Wims first learned baseball from his father, Jim, who owned the farm on which the baseball diamond was located. Jim sacrificed this portion he could have used to grow crops so that his six children could have a place to play outside. It was here that Wilson

*Left*: An older Wilson Wims sits on his deck at home in Clarksburg. *Frances Barnhart.*

*Opposite*: The Rockville Colored High School Baseball Team, circa 1932. Russell Awkard (*kneeling, first from right*) went on to play in the Negro National League. *MCHS.*

Wims would play for the Hyattstown Bluebirds and, later, coach the highly successful Maryland Wildcats.

Founded and owned by Wims, the Wildcats were one of the first Black sandlot baseball teams in the early twentieth century. The team won thirty-seven games in a row in 1952 and sent many of its players to the professional Negro leagues. Despite the Wildcats' obvious talent, most teammates were kept from Major League Baseball by segregation. Notable teammates included Chuck Hinton, an outfielder for the Cleveland Indians, and Sonny Jackson, who became a shortstop and later a coach for the Atlanta Braves.

After the Negro leagues were phased out, Wims sponsored the integrated Junior Wildcats. Family friend Ethel Gardiner Frye recalled one unforgettable moment of Wims's coaching career in 1970, when one of his White players came off the field devastated because he had struck out twice. Frye writes in *A Remarkable Life* about the pep talk Wims gave to the teary-eyed boy. "Don't worry about it, Babe Ruth strikes out, you know?" he told him. The next time the boy went up to bat, he came back crying not because he had struck out again but because he was so overjoyed about the home run he had just scored.

Wims's beloved reputation extended beyond Wims Meadow to the community of Clarksburg. In February 1952, a snowstorm stranded a busload of schoolchildren as they tried to head home from Rocky Hill Elementary School. Wims and his wife, Sarah, took in all thirty of the children and let them stay overnight at his house across the street until they could be transported home.

Wims was a prominent builder and community leader in Montgomery County, spearheading the construction of Clarksburg's recreation center, Rockville's Lincoln Park housing project and the expansion of Scotland

Church in Bethesda. He made a special effort to create housing for Black families who could not typically afford to live outside of Washington, D.C. Using what Frye calls a "rent-to-own" model, he allowed these families to rent his homes along Wims Road in Clarksburg until they could afford to buy their property, at which point he would sell it off to them.

In 2008, ninety-two-year-old Wims threw out the first pitch at Clarksburg High School's new baseball field, Wims Field, named in his honor. On August 25, 2014, six months after Wims's passing at the age of ninety-eight, Wilson Wims Elementary School welcomed students for the first time. And of course, the elementary school's mascot is the Wildcat.

Chapter 11

# Joe Acanfora vs. MCPS

## *A Case Study of the Gay Rights Movement*

When I got on the phone with Joe Acanfora one August afternoon, his cheerfulness immediately caught my attention. And why not? He's retired, he lives in a wonderful community in the East Bay area of San Francisco and in just nine days, he was scheduled to leave for two months to tour Europe with his husband, Hai.

He has a country house in Mendocino, plenty of gardening and housework to keep him productive and financial stability from his pension and his and Hai's home-cooking business that they sell from one day a week. At seventy-three years old, Acanfora gets to live and love comfortably with the support of neighbors, good friends and family in a city that has been called the "LGBTQ capital of the world." It hasn't always been this way, especially in 1972, when he came to Rockville, Maryland, to teach science at Parkland Junior High School. Just over a month later, his teaching career would be finished.

Long before he landed in the Washington, D.C. area, he had a promising start in Bricktown, New Jersey, where he graduated from Brick Township High School as valedictorian. He went on to Penn State University on an NROTC scholarship and studied secondary science education. Acanfora seemed to have a bright future ahead of him, but something was keeping him from fully enjoying his prospects.

Since the age of twelve or thirteen, he'd known he was gay. "I was upset and depressed about not being 'normal' in the '60s." Acanfora said. "Back then, there was so much censorship on homosexuality. It was called 'sexual perversion.'"

Without any information available in libraries, in school or in the media, and without the existence of the internet, Acanfora searched for resources about being gay but had little luck. He struggled to find a reason to go on living. After dealing with enough frustration and suicidal thoughts at Penn State, he came out to the university psychiatrist, telling him that he just wanted to meet one other gay person on campus. The psychiatrist told Acanfora that he couldn't endorse putting him in touch with another homosexual. "There's an alley in downtown State College," the psychiatrist suggested. "Maybe you can try and meet someone there."

Although the Penn State administration did not support his homosexuality, Acanfora found support when he told his parents soon after. They did not fully understand the revelation, but they supported him completely as long as he was happy and healthy. His father would later shake his hand and tell him, "I loved you then and I love you now."

Acanfora's life at school had started to become much more bearable. His luck changed in 1970 when he found an index card in the school cafeteria advertising a meeting to help those "with questions about homosexuality." The group, the Homophiles of Penn State, grew from five or six people in its first meeting to twenty to thirty members that year. Through consistent backlash from the university, HOPS held forums to educate students about the gay community and eventually sponsored gay social events. "It was the first acknowledgment I had that there was another gay person in the world," Acanfora said. "And then I got to be treasurer of one of the first gay student organizations in the country."

Joe Acanfora with his mother, Leonore Acanfora. *Joe Acanfora.*

In 1972, Acanfora graduated from Penn State with a bachelor's degree in secondary science education and was ready to go out and teach, but there was one huge problem. For Acanfora to receive his teaching certification in Pennsylvania, the dean of Penn State's College of Education would have to perform a routine sign-off on Acanfora's "good moral character." That April, the dean refused to sign off on his application, instead convening the University Teacher Certification Council to help him decide on the fate of the "avowed homosexual" student.

As his certification kept being delayed and was eventually sent up to be decided by the Pennsylvania secretary of education, Acanfora continued his job hunt amid campus protests by students fighting for his certification. In Maryland, he came across as a traditional candidate with a new bachelor's degree in secondary education. The state granted him a certification to teach there, and his professional life was about to begin.

On August 29, 1972, Joe Acanfora started work as Mr. Acanfora, eighth grade earth science teacher at Parkland Junior High School in Rockville. "My boyfriend from Penn State and I moved to D.C., near Dupont Circle. I commuted to Parkland," Acanfora recalled. "I loved living there. The school was very nice. It was a really pleasant, enjoyable job situation. The students were good. I enjoyed teaching there."

In the next few weeks, Acanfora would start to find his footing in Washington. With his simple routine of going to school, then coming home to his boyfriend at the time, he seemed to have gotten far enough away from the discrimination he faced in Pennsylvania.

The last week and a half of September 1972 came with both good news and bad news for Acanfora. On September 22, Pennsylvania secretary of education John C. Pittenger called a press conference to announce that he had certified Acanfora to teach in the state of Pennsylvania. The news of the first openly gay man certified to teach in Pennsylvania traveled quickly through major outlets like the *New York Times* and the *Philadelphia Inquirer*. "The resolution of the Pennsylvania certification in the *Washington Post* brought about the trouble at Parkland," Acanfora said.

On September 26, Acanfora received a letter from the deputy superintendent of Montgomery County Public Schools, indicating that they were aware of the case in Pennsylvania and that he would be "temporarily" transferred away from working with students to the Department of Curriculum and Instruction. MCPS also informed him that he was not allowed to enter Parkland or be around the children.

In yet another fight for his career, Acanfora filed a lawsuit against MCPS to return to his job in the classroom. With the support of his friends, family and the National Education Association, Acanfora found much greater motivation to fight against the unjust firing disguised as a transfer. "There was one manager at my job who wouldn't vouch for my moral character in the lawsuit because he didn't want to lose his job. The friendship ended," Acanfora said, "but there were so many letters and so much support for me. It was so much easier to fight discrimination because of all the support, a relatively easier battle to fight than the one I struggled with internally before 'coming out.'"

Joe Acanfora at his apartment in the winter of 1972. *Joe Acanfora.*

Throughout 1972 and 1973, local TV stations invited Acanfora to share his story. He appeared on Maury Povich's local Washington show *Panorama* and New York Public Television's *How Do Your Children Grow?* Then one day, CBS showed up at Acanfora's home in Dupont Circle. "Morley Safer came to interview me at my apartment, and I thought, 'Wow, this has become a much bigger deal than I could have imagined!'" Acanfora said. "Rewatching that episode, it was a pivotal moment in my personal self-acceptance, but also my clothes were embarrassing-looking back then."

The episode of *60 Minutes* aired on February 25, 1973, as "The Case of Joe Acanfora." Parkland students, their parents and teachers gave their thoughts on the firing. In an interview with three of the Parkland teachers, one female teacher stated that when the professional staff sent a petition around saying that Acanfora's firing was unjust, sixty-one out of eighty-three teachers signed in agreement. They further elaborated that he had positive and moral objectives as a teacher and was a "nice fella."

A group of Acanfora's students, who were unaware of their teacher's homosexuality until the news reached Washington, also started a petition to reinstate Acanfora after their school counselor would not give them a reasonable explanation for why he was fired. The children tried to submit their petition to the D.C. Board of Education but were ignored. "There were two kids in the class who were rowdy nuisances and troublemakers. After I was taken out, both of them were two of my strongest advocates: they were interviewed by *60 Minutes* and were extremely supportive," Acanfora chuckled.

The parents of Parkland students were more split on the matter. Some appreciated Acanfora for the good influence he had on their children's interest in learning science, saying that his sexuality had no effect on his teaching ability and that his private life should be respected. Others sided with MCPS, discussing their fears of a homosexual modeling improper behavior in the classroom or forming inappropriate bonds with their children. Acanfora affirmed, "I have to be honest with myself, and other people can live a separate life, live a dual life, hiding from everyone the fact that they're gay, but that's just… I think it's playing a game, and I don't know how healthy that is."

The year 1973 would be a vindicating but maddening one for Acanfora. In January, his old student organization, HOPS, was finally granted a student organization charter by Penn State after almost two years of fighting for recognition. That April, two months after the *60 Minutes* broadcast, students, staff, school officials, pediatricians and psychiatrists joined Acanfora at the federal district court in Baltimore to testify as witnesses in the courtroom. The trial lasted for four days before the court began deliberating on Acanfora's case.

Another letter came for him on May 1. MCPS had spoken again: they would not be renewing his employment contract, ending not only his time in the classroom but also his work in the Department of Curriculum and Instruction. Meanwhile, the district court was still deciding whether Acanfora's firing was justified. Would the court be able to save his teaching career?

The news was a mix of bad and good when the district court came back with its decision on May 31. The court ultimately refused to let Acanfora return to MCPS. "The reason I ultimately lost," he elaborated, "was that the administration and courts and legal system were prejudiced. They did say, 'Gay teachers are now a protected class and cannot be fired for being gay,' but they said I abused my discretion as a teacher for talking about it openly on *60 Minutes*."

The following month, Acanfora filed an appeal of the district court's decision in the United States Court of Appeals for the Fourth Circuit. Another eight months went by, yielding similar results. On February 7, 1974, the court issued an opinion that his public statements on *60 Minutes* were protected by the First Amendment since speech regarding homosexuality was a "matter of public concern." But the opinion came with a twist.

While it disagreed with the lower court's reasoning, the circuit court did affirm the district court's decision on different grounds. In *Acanfora vs. Board of Education of Montgomery County* (1974), the court ruled that "he is not entitled to relief because of material omissions in his application for a teaching position." Two court cases later, he remained out of the classroom. "At the appeals level, they said I had lied on my teaching application by not putting down 'gay activism' as an extracurricular activity, so I 'falsified' my application," Acanfora said.

In the year when most Americans were focused on the Supreme Court case against President Nixon, Acanfora set his mind on the hope that this court would hear his case, too. That summer, he filed an appeal to the Supreme Court, but in the fall of 1974, his writ of certiorari was denied. His long fight against the school system had ended in favor of the opposition.

The battle to be recognized as a gay educator took a toll on Acanfora. "It took me a few years to regroup," Acanfora said. "The lawsuits and being openly gay hindered me. I had to figure out how to get income since I couldn't find a teaching job."

Acanfora demonstrated a stubborn determination during his three years fighting the government that helped carry him past the consequences of the discrimination suits. While his suspension from the Department of Curriculum and Instruction may have seemed like an unfair punishment in 1972, Acanfora later used his experience writing curriculum documents there to land a job working for the government in research and grants administration. He found a new community with friends and coworkers at local gay bars and with the Gay Activist Alliance of Washington. He later bought a house in Avondale, a neighborhood in Chillum, Maryland.

Things began to look up for Acanfora, and while he wondered if there were things he could have said or done differently to win his case, he continued to fight for LGBTQ rights in the 1980s. A new grants and contract management job at the University of California, Berkeley, brought him to the San Francisco area, where he fought against California's civil propositions to keep homosexual teachers out of the classroom. Acanfora also became treasurer of the East Bay Lesbian & Gay Democratic Club. As a leader of the organization, he helped the City of Oakland pass an ordinance to prevent discrimination based on sexual orientation. While he lost his court battles on the East Coast, he took the courage he gained from these experiences and went on to make even greater progress for LGBTQ rights on the West Coast.

Today, Acanfora looks back proudly on the battle he fought and lost in the courts fifty years ago. "Overall, I have no regrets," he said. "It was one of the most momentous times in my life, I did something good for young gay people. I think I probably educated more people in those three years of court about issues important for young students than I would have as a junior high school science teacher."

In the years since his legal battle, Acanfora said he has received numerous letters and Facebook requests from old and young people who have been inspired by his case. In one letter Acanfora received in 2012, a man thanked him for defiantly coming out and fighting MCPS's decision. As a teenager in Montgomery County watching coverage of Acanfora's case, he struggled less with accepting his own homosexuality than he might have without Acanfora's confident example.

Since Acanfora moved out of the area, MCPS has become much more progressive in how it treats members of the LGBTQ community. Rockville's newest elementary school opened in 2018 under the name Bayard Rustin Elementary School, honoring the late gay activist who closely advised Martin Luther King Jr. during the civil rights movement. In the fall of 2021, the first LGBTQ studies class was offered to MCPS students as a semester-long, half-credit social studies class. In August 2023, a federal district court ruled that certain LGBTQ-themed texts could be allowed in the MCPS curriculum.

While these advancements might sound encouraging to Acanfora, he still would like a formal apology from MCPS. "An apology would formally recognize that MCPS did the wrong thing; it would send a message to the kids today who are struggling," Acanfora said. "It would be meaningful to me, and more importantly, it would establish a clear record for the gay kids today that anti-gay discrimination is wrong—both then and now—and that gay students and teachers are worthy members of our community."

Chapter 12

# THE GROWTH AND STRENGTH
# OF MOCO'S JEWISH COMMUNITY

Across the entire United States, less than 3 percent of the population identifies as Jewish. Change that scope to just Montgomery County, and you'll find that number jumps to around 10 percent. With representation like this, it's not hard to see that MoCo has become a center of growth for the Jewish population. But we weren't always this welcoming.

Prior to the twentieth century, it is hard to find much evidence of Jews living in Montgomery County. Much of the county was still rural and not yet known for the diverse population it has today. The small village of Slidell near Boyds did have one well-known Jewish family living there in 1899. Postmaster Louis Rosenstein had moved with his wife, Dora, into the post office there, where they operated a small but successful general store, which imported products from Baltimore, Frederick and Washington. The couple had immigrated from Russia to Baltimore and then came to Slidell during the early 1890s.

Tragedy struck on May 13, 1899, when a local Black man named Armistead Taylor robbed the store and brutally murdered Louis and Dora, who was reported to be several months pregnant at the time. As the *Evening Star* reported on May 15, the Rosensteins' sad and furious neighbors demanded justice for the deaths of the "thrifty Hebrews." Taylor was later tracked to Georgetown, where he killed a police sergeant before surrendering. His uncle John Brown was, controversially, charged as a coconspirator in the crime. Three months later, Taylor and Brown were hanged in Rockville for the killings.

Per the 1900 U.S. census, only a few Jewish families made their homes in Montgomery County then. The Fox, Stearman and Goldberg families were all merchant families, while Benjamin Lenovitz supported his family by operating a grocery store in Rockville. The Foxes lived in Poolesville, the Stearmans in Wheaton, the Goldbergs in Laytonsville and the Lenovitzes in Norbeck. All four families were listed as originating from Russia, and all four had evidently left Montgomery County by the 1910 census.

As more Jewish families moved to MoCo for federal government jobs, they struggled with severe residential and recreational discrimination. In 1913, the Washington Suburban Club was founded by Washingtonian Jews who were not allowed to join other golf or country clubs because of their ethnicity. Today, this club is known as Woodmont Country Club in Rockville. President Woodrow Wilson, comedian Bob Hope and singer Kate Smith are just a few of its notable guests from the last eleven decades.

Jews who wanted to live in Montgomery County faced housing covenants that kept them from moving into many neighborhoods during the early twentieth century. Jewish real estate developers like Sam Eig, Morris Cafritz and Abraham Kay built up neighborhoods like Rock Creek Forest and Indian Spring in Silver Spring so their community could have a place to live. Kemp Mill, which was heavily developed by Abraham Kay's son, Jack, currently has one of the largest Orthodox Jewish populations in the United States.

In 1948, the Supreme Court ruled in *Shelley v. Kraemer* that restrictive property covenants were unenforceable. In 1968, the passage of the Fair Housing Act offered broader protections, much greater public exposure to housing discrimination and a system for violated parties to file complaints through the Department of Housing and Urban Development. Although developers like Eig, Cafritz and Kay had faced discrimination as Jewish people themselves, they used similarly unfair tactics toward people of color by restricting them from living in their primarily Caucasian and Jewish neighborhoods. Eventually, after the Fair Housing Act came into effect, they were practically forced to treat every housing candidate equally.

After World War II, the local Jewish population skyrocketed and the first Jewish congregations came to Montgomery County. In 1952, the Montgomery County Jewish Community Group broke ground on its first synagogue, what would later be known as Congregation Ohr Kodesh in Chevy Chase. The future Ohr Kodesh's construction was led by Sam Eig, and it became the first synagogue in Maryland south of Baltimore.

Local developer Abraham S. Kay (*right*) shakes hands with U.S. ambassador to Israel James G. McDonald (*left*) at an event in Washington, D.C., circa 1950s. *United States Holocaust Memorial Museum, courtesy of Jack Kay.*

An early sketch of Montgomery County Jewish Community Center, now known as Congregation Ohr Kodesh in Chevy Chase. Construction began in 1952. *MCHS.*

Sam Eig was born in 1898 in Minsk, Belarus, and immigrated to the United States in 1914, fleeing the outbreak of World War I. According to his grandson, Michael Eig, fifteen-year-old Sam dreamed of going out to Nebraska to be a cowboy. He stopped in Washington, D.C., to work and save up money for life in the West but ended up staying in Washington to become a successful real estate developer. Aside from churches, synagogues and neighborhoods, Eig built up the Shady Grove Music Fair and the Washingtonian Country Club in Gaithersburg. After his death in 1982, the extension of I-370 from I-270 to Great Seneca Highway was named Sam Eig Highway in his honor.

Many of the Jewish residents who came to Montgomery County had survived the Holocaust, suffering terribly in the process. Flora Mendelowicz Singer was one of them. As a Jewish child in Belgium, she had witnessed the banishment of her people from local shops and parks, deliberate burning of her synagogue and the deportation of her extended family and neighbors to concentration camps. In a 1989 interview for the Holocaust Eyewitness Project, Singer noted that her entire immediate family was lucky to escape deportation without having to pay someone to protect them. From 1942 until Belgium was liberated from the Nazis in 1944, she and her family were hidden with the help of figures like a school principal and the nuns at a Catholic convent.

Shortly after the liberation, Flora Singer writes in her notebook while attending a Catholic school in Brussels, Belgium, circa 1945. *United States Holocaust Memorial Museum, courtesy of Flora Mendelowicz Singer.*

Singer came to the United States in 1946, eventually settling in Potomac and becoming well known in the Montgomery County Public School system as a foreign language teacher. In 1985, she coauthored a highly successful course for MCPS on how to teach the sensitive topic of the Holocaust. Three years after her death in 2009, Flora M. Singer Elementary School in Silver Spring was opened and named after her.

According to the Jewish Federation of Greater Washington, MoCo had forty Jewish congregations, twenty-three Jewish preschools and ten Jewish day schools as of 2023. I'll put it another way: if you're a seventh grader at Robert Frost Middle School, like I was, you're almost guaranteed to see or wear a new sweatshirt every Monday from the bar or bat mitzvah that happened over the weekend.

PART III

THE OTHER SIDE OF MoCo

Chapter 13

# WHAT A WAY TO GO

## *Dramatic Deaths with Crazy Causes*

In a word, I would describe this chapter as "morbid." Take it more as a warning than a description. If you're fascinated by old-timey deaths mixed with some *Final Destination*–esque details, don't skip this chapter.

Our first story takes place at a wedding hosted by the Waters family in the Woodside neighborhood of Silver Spring on April 3, 1919. George and Mary Waters were celebrating the marriage of their daughter, eighteen-year-old Linda Waters, to twenty-one-year-old Frank Willson. After the ceremony, friends and family enjoyed refreshments along with Frank and Linda. The big event had gone off successfully, and the guests enjoyed the festivities as the evening continued.

Then—chaos. As Linda carried on in her bridal garb, she failed to notice that she had passed too close to a lighted candle and her veil was now on fire. Quickly, the veil was torn from her head and thrown to the floor. Linda and the rest of the partygoers should have been able to breathe a sigh of relief, but in the commotion, no one bothered to think where on the floor that fiery veil would land. And it landed right at the feet of Elizabeth Willson, the groom's fifteen-year-old sister.

Elizabeth had no chance to dodge the veil, and the flames quickly engulfed her in her dress made of highly inflammable material. Several men in the room threw off their coats and tried to suffocate the blaze, but the girl's clothes had been burned away, and she was gravely injured.

Although she lingered through the severe burns on her arms and face, Elizabeth contracted a septic infection two days after the accident and died

Elizabeth Earl Willson's grave at Sandy Spring Meetinghouse Cemetery. *Author's collection*.

at the Willson family home in Layhill on April 6, 1919. Despite the traumatic start to their marriage, Linda and Frank raised three children and remained married for almost sixty-two years until Linda's death in 1981.

While Elizabeth's gravestone in Sandy Spring Friends Meetinghouse Cemetery is a simple one, the coverage of her death was not only tragic but also unsettling. On page 3 of the *Sentinel*'s April 11, 1919 edition, there is the obituary explaining the accidental death of Elizabeth Willson at Frank and Linda's wedding. But look three columns over on the same page and what do you see? A wedding announcement for Frank and Linda, listing Elizabeth as a bridesmaid and summing up the tragedy with: "Following the ceremony, a large reception was held, the couple leaving later for an extended trip." Was it a horrific accident or a lovely wedding? The *Sentinel* seemed to say both.

Perhaps Elizabeth watched Frank and Linda live out their married years after all, or at least she could watch anyone who lived in the house where she caught fire. In her book with Karen Yaffe Lottes, *In Search of Maryland Ghosts: Montgomery County*, Dorothy Pugh describes how years later, the new owners of the Waters home felt "strange sensations" there and called in a psychic. The psychic noticed a chilly wind throughout the house, most intensely felt in the dining room where the tragedy occurred. She turned to the people who lived there and told them that certainly, there was a ghost among them.

The community of Layhill didn't catch much of a break at the turn of the twentieth century. Yet another freak accident occurred on June 1, 1897: the death of nine-year-old Jessie Connelly. Jessie and her friends were walking back from school that afternoon when they decided to pay a visit to the Atwood family at their general store. The children were welcomed by Mr. and Mrs. Atwood. As Jessie sat on Mrs. Atwood's lap, the Atwoods' playful but naive seven-year-old son appeared with his father's rifle, exclaiming, "I will shoot you!" before firing a bullet into the girl's forehead.

Like fellow Layhill resident Elizabeth Willson, Jessie fought remarkably in her condition, surviving for more than two days before succumbing to her wounds on June 3, 1897. Apparently, no charges were brought against the boy or his parents, who went on to have six more children after the shooting.

In the early twentieth century, freak fatalities occurred for various reasons. If you were farmer William Penn of Redland, you died from a blow to the head when one of your hay bales fell off your wagon and crushed you. If you were mail carrier Trovilla Duvall of Boyds, you got lost in a rainstorm looking for your livestock and were swept away when Seneca Creek flooded

On March 19, 1936, Seneca Creek flooded Riverside Inn at Seneca. Another Seneca Creek flood had taken the life of twenty-one-year-old Trovilla Duvall in 1908. *MCHS.*

its banks. Even an undercooked meal could be a death sentence in 1922, when food poisoning from a can of spareribs killed fourteen-month-old Eleanor Bussard of Neelsville and put two of her siblings in critical condition.

Although emerging technologies have saved lives, labor and time over the past century, a couple locals also lost their lives due to their inadequacies. There was thirteen-year-old Helen Lawrence, who, in 1908, went to visit her grandmother at the Washington Sanitarium in Takoma Park while she was infirm with "nervousness." While the usual operator went on lunch break, Mrs. Irwin, the matron of the hospital, operated the elevator for Helen, a woman called Mrs. Whitehead and Mrs. Whitehead's eleven-year-old son. Mrs. Irwin noticed that the car was descending slowly and decided to get out at the basement of the shaft to check out the mechanism.

After she exited the car, the crank-operated elevator inexplicably began to ascend. Mrs. Whitehead and her son jumped out of the car and onto the basement floor to safety in time, but Helen hesitated, diving too late, and was crushed between the elevator floor and the basement ceiling. The girl's screaming and the Whiteheads' frantic cries brought over the hospital staff, who lowered the elevator and rushed Helen's now unconscious body into the operating room.

Helen's mother, Gracia, hurried down from Baltimore to see her. Helen regained consciousness and initially didn't seem to be seriously injured, but as the night went on, she became weaker and weaker, finally passing on seven hours after receiving her injuries.

What or who caused the crank to lift the elevator? The hospital claimed that one of the two children in the elevator must have been messing with the crank and moved it from the stop position, although neither Helen nor the Whitehead boy ever admitted it. Either way, it didn't matter. The hospital and Helen's family accepted that the death was an accident, and apparently, no charges were ever brought against the Washington Sanitarium for Helen's death.

For Gaithersburg's Mayor Richard H. Miles, it was doing a good deed for his community that led to his demise. Every morning, Mayor Miles would drive over to the electric switch house to turn off the currents to the city's streetlights as daylight arrived. One August morning in 1918, local bank clerk John Stover noticed that Miles's car was parked outside the switch house with the motor running. Curious, Stover investigated the switch house and found the badly charred body of Mayor Miles, who had been electrocuted by a live current.

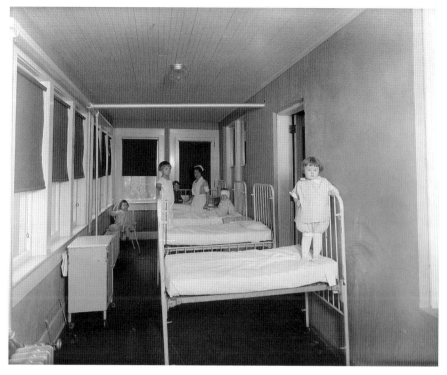

A nurse tends to the children at Washington Sanitarium in Takoma Park, circa 1920s. In 1908, thirteen-year-old Helen Lawrence died here in a tragic accident. *LOC.*

You would think that a mayor's sudden and violent death would be enough to make the front page of the *Montgomery County Sentinel*, but that wasn't the case here. Many local readers discovered news of Mayor Miles' demise in a lightly bolded section on page 3 of the August 9, 1918, edition, under the concise headline "Mayor Miles Accidentally Killed."

More than one hundred years later, getting fatally poisoned by a can of food or crushed by a malfunctioning elevator seems like a worry of the past. Did the universe have some intricate design to kill these unfortunate Montgomery Countians? Let's pay our respects to those mentioned in this chapter and pray we go more peacefully.

Chapter 14

# A County Full of Ghosts

Whether you think they're real or all a bunch of woo-woo folk tales, ghost stories can be entertaining, especially when they involve someone or somewhere close to you.

The Little Falls of the Potomac River cascade at the Washington, D.C. border near Brookmont, Maryland. Back in 1873, an old fisherman wrote a story for the *Montgomery County Sentinel*, recounting the tale of the little drummer boy who haunts the shores of Little Falls.

The fisherman's tale appeared in the *Sentinel* on June 20, 1873, and told of a British army marching its way north during the "Indian wars" more than one hundred years earlier. They had made their way up from Virginia and were headed to the Great Lakes. When it came time to cross the Potomac at Little Falls, the men climbed into their boat to ferry themselves across the river to the tune of their beloved drummer boy's drum. In the process, the drummer boy accidentally fell into the water. With the drum around his neck, he was unable to pull himself up, so he drowned.

The soldiers sadly marched on, unable to wipe the sound of the drum from their memory. According to the fisherman, the boy's drum could still be heard in the Potomac valley, often during the Revolutionary War and by the fisherman himself more than one hundred times. The old man continued:

> *But what was very strange, whenever that phantom drum was heard, the river was sure to bring up from its depths the body of some man who had been drowned. It was thought by many that the man who first heard the*

*pealing of this strange sound was sure to lose his life by drowning before the coming morrow.*

Are all ghosts out to get us? Apparently not, according to Germantown resident Terry LaMotte. Growing up in Olde Towne Gaithersburg, she had pleasant experiences in her childhood home with previous owners Samuel and Lelia Briggs. While they were living in this Victorian house, Samuel was a dairy farmer and Lelia was an avid gardener. "We had Mr. and Mrs. Briggs with us in the house on Park Avenue," LaMotte said. "I remember seeing an apparition of Mrs. Briggs walking in my room. She was sort of floating, with a long, flowing gown, dark hair in a bun, carrying a candle. I don't remember seeing any feet."

When LaMotte's stepfather saw Mrs. Briggs for the first time, he didn't think much about her at first because he thought she was LaMotte's mother. The Briggs ghosts were benevolent to LaMotte's family—but like most humans, the LaMottes had their limits. "One night, we set our friends up in the room that used to be theirs," she said. "Our guests had an argument, and the Briggses appeared. After that, our friends spent the rest of the night sleeping on the front porch."

LaMotte now lives near Butler's Orchard in Germantown, but her family still experiences the paranormal. "My daughter started having nightmares. There were things sitting on her chest," LaMotte said. "We had a priest and my friend Laine, a medium, come over. We had a family of four in our closet that told Laine to 'get out.' And the Native American ghosts on our property warned us not to go to the open part of our land for fear of us getting shot."

Terry LaMotte's daughter discovered this 1817 Liberty Head coin while walking near their home in Germantown. *Terry LaMotte.*

While searching for a property marker, LaMotte's daughter found a Liberty Head penny from 1817. And in the park behind their property, she found a stone with a cross marker. "We thought this was a slave marker, but it turns out it was a soldier who died retreating from Monocacy in the Civil War," LaMotte said.

Laine Crosby recalls becoming suddenly psychic after moving to a haunted eighteenth-century plantation in Derwood. Since then, she has become known as a best-selling author and investigative medium, working with authors, historians, archaeologists and

*Left*: Boblitt caught an eerie, perhaps ghostly, orb in this picture. The photo was taken in 2011, shortly after Boblitt bought the old house at Woodstock. *Mary-Margaret Boblitt.*

*Below*: The eerie orb appears on Boblitt's dog, George—aptly named after George Washington. *M. Boblitt.*

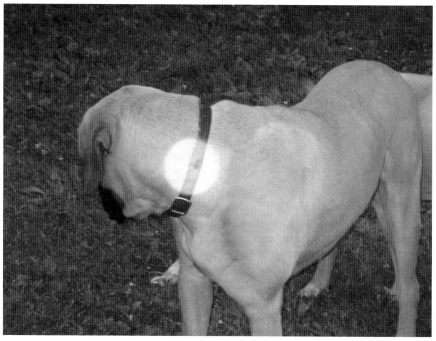

law enforcement to find out what history hasn't revealed. "There's a lot of activity at sites like the Josiah Henson Museum and Little Bennett Regional Park," Crosby said. "Up in Brookeville, too, there are so many ghost kids at Oakley Cabin. It's a happy place; they always want to take me to a stream to play."

Remember Woodstock Manor, where George Washington had a tenant house? Owner Mary-Margaret Boblitt has some stories, too. Up until a few years ago, she says, she kept having run-ins with the paranormal. In one instance, she and her mother, Susan, were downstairs when they heard the resident dogs barking and a woman telling them "Be quiet!" twice in succession. They figured that this was their friend who was staying with them at the time, but when the friend pulled into the driveway an hour later and said she had been out at a festival for the past few hours, Mary-Margaret and her mom started to wonder.

Further strange activity in the house has consisted of usually docile dogs barking ferociously at random corners of the room, visitors having their shirts tugged by unseen forces, old artifacts levitating above the refrigerator and previous owners hearing children laughing and playing. Once, Boblitt woke up and was about to leave her bed when she heard the voice of a little girl ask, "Are you breathing?"

Then there was that one time with the ceiling fan. The previous owners had left a ceiling fan in one of the upstairs rooms that was broken, so Boblitt had disconnected it from its power source. "There was plastic on the windows in the room because we were doing work on the house. There was no wind that day, but as I came up the stairs, I saw the plastic was billowing," Boblitt recalled. "I look up, and this fan, which hadn't worked for eight or nine years, was going at Mach 10 speed. It slowed down and stopped as soon as I got to the top of the stairs."

From stories of guardian spirits in the chimney to top-hatted apparitions floating above the pillow at night, Woodstock may be the most haunted property in MoCo yet. During various visits from "energy workers," as Boblitt calls them, she has heard claims about why her house is haunted. One said that her house was a "vortex" for the ghosts, referring to it as a "speakeasy for the dead." The investigator also told Boblitt that most of the ghosts hang out in her kitchen and think she's rude because she doesn't say good morning to them. Boblitt responded, "The day I say good morning and they respond, I'll burn the house down and leave."

Chapter 15

# THE TORNADO THAT CAME TO LAYTONSVILLE

I remember hiding out for only one tornado warning as a little kid in Gaithersburg. My parents gave my siblings and me the cue one evening to head down to the basement, away from any windows. *We should be scared*, I thought, *but why do I feel excited?* The cautious part of my brain wanted to stay inside, safe and huddled together with my family, while the adventurous part wanted to sprint out into the heavy winds and see if I could spot my first funnel cloud from the backyard.

Reading up on the following story is one reason why I no longer experience this sensation.

In 1929, the worst tornado in Montgomery County history took the lives of three people near Laytonsville and one person in Brookeville. This tragedy was part of a larger devastation known as the Rye Cove tornado outbreak, which killed at least forty-two people and injured more than three hundred. On May 1 and 2, an outbreak of cyclones tore through the South from Oklahoma to Maryland.

It rained. It hailed. It thundered. Lightning struck. The night of May 2, 1929, must have been a terrifying time for many up-county residents. Winds came in at an F3 rating on the Fujita scale, which the National Weather Service describes as a "severe tornado" moving between 158 and 206 miles per hour. During an F3 tornado, it is typical for well-constructed houses to have their roofs and walls torn off. F3 events have also been known to overturn trains and uproot most of the trees in a forest.

On May 10, 1929, an article in the *Montgomery County Sentinel* called "Storm Devastation in the County" recounted the tragedy. Near Brookeville, Charles F. Haight and his wife, Clara, were sitting on the first floor of their two-hundred-year-old home when the twister blasted apart their stone walls and blew the couple outside through a giant hole onto their lawn. Charles and Clara survived the blast but could not find Clara's mother, who had been upstairs. Mounting a horse, Charles rode through the harsh rain and winds seeking assistance. He managed to round up a team of volunteers from Roxbury Mills, just over the Patuxent River into Howard County. The volunteers came down to the Haight property to help sort through the debris, eventually discovering and retrieving the body of Charles' eighty-eight-year-old mother-in-law, Amelia Knapp.

In the tiny community of Grifton, the tornado wrecked J. William Benson's entire farm. Every building on the property was obliterated, more than one hundred trees were uprooted and his expansive, profitable apple orchard was destroyed. Benson resided in Rockville and had recently leased the farm to a family that was scheduled to move in that same week. Luckily, the prospective tenants had not moved in yet, but they lost the furniture they had already set up in their doomed new home.

In the Laytonsville district, there would not be such luck. When the tornado hit the home of farmer F. Bowie Childs, all seven residents had gone to bed. The twister blew down every building except the barn. Bowie; his wife, Mollie; three of their four children; Bowie's mother, Octavia; and a farmhand named James Leizear were battered and beaten during the storm.

People from all over Montgomery County came to look at the destruction left by the tornado. Seen here are the ruins of the Benson farm. *Photo by Lewis Reed, courtesy of Jeanne Gartner.*

4 *          THE EVENING ST

# DEVASTATION WROUGHT B

## TORNADOES STRIKE NEAR WASHINGTON

### 11 Killed, 19 Hurt in Maryland and Virginia Towns Around Capital.

(Continued From First Page.)

L. Wachter, near Harmony Grove, lacerated.

Mrs. Martin L. Wachter, bruised and shock.

Miss Dorothy Doll, 17, near Frederick, cut about face and limbs.

Miss Helen McGlow, 18, near Frederick, shock.

The home of Shank, a two-story frame building, was demolished and the timbers scattered several hundred yards. Mrs. Shank's body was found about 150 feet from the foundation of the building. Shank, unconscious, was found by his wife's side. He died at the Frederick City Hospital early this morning.

Mr. and Mrs. Fout occupied Richfield, the birthplace of the late Admiral Winfield Scott Schley, naval hero of the Spanish-American War, near Harmony Grove, which was badly damaged by the storm. Mr. and Mrs. Fout were in a second-story bedroom when the tornado hit. They were injured about the face and body. They were taken to the hospital, but their condition is not considered serious.

#### Windows Are Blown In.

Mr. and Mrs. Wachter received lacerations about the face and hands, when windows of their home on the farm of Thomas Hayward, near Harmony Grove, blew in. They were taken to the hospital and released.

The home of Mr. and Mrs. Frank Doll, near Frederick, was wrecked and their daughter, Miss Dorothy Doll, and a friend, Miss Helen McGlow, were injured. Mr. and Mrs. Doll and members of the household were asleep when the storm struck. The two girls were removed from their beds after the room had fallen about them. Neither was injured seriously.

The residence of Evan C. Biser, near Frederick, was damaged. The barn near the house was wrecked.

At Mount Pleasant the tornado cut a narrow path through the town and demolished the barn, garage and outbuildings of Millard Crum. The wind swept through the property of William Burrier and uprooted two rows of mature apple trees in the orchard of Wilbur Smith, a neighbor.

#### Rail Tracks Washed Out.

All that was left of the home of William H. Childs, near Laytonsville, Md., after the torna noon. Three members of the family met death.

The home of Pete Laws at Catlett, Va., near Warrenton, Va. Five persons lost their lives i them.

From the *Evening Star*, May 3, 1929: William Childs (*top right photo*) visits the ruins of his family's home on May 3, 1929. Childs lost two siblings and his grandmother in the tornado. *Reprinted with permission of the DC Public Library, Star Collection © Washington Post.*

SHINGTON, D. C., FRIDAY, MAY 3, 1929.

# TORNADO IN NEARBY COMM

esterday after-
ar Staff Photo.

Left to right: William Childs and Paul Groshen, photographed in the ruins of the Childs' home.—Star Staff Photo.

a, Laws among
ar Staff Photo.

Another view of the Laws' home. Two twisters hit this area and the countryside this morning was strewn with the bodies of dead chickens, horses and cows.
—Star Staff Photo.

Leizear managed to endure the chaos, pulling himself out of the wreckage and running half a mile to a neighbor's house to call for help.

It took three fire departments from Gaithersburg, Sandy Spring and Rockville to sort through the destruction. Firemen discovered the bodies of eighty-six-year-old Octavia and eight-year-old Florence Childs buried under the rubble. The rest of the family were transported to Montgomery General Hospital, where Dr. Jacob W. Bird administered to their injuries. According to a *Washington Times* article from the day after the event, the victims suffered from bruises, shock and lacerations. In addition, Bowie Childs sustained a fractured arm.

Bowie, Mollie, their seventeen-year-old son Fielder and Leizear would recover from and survive the ordeal. The morning after the tornado, twenty-year-old Hampton Childs died in the hospital. The brutal storm had thrown him three hundred feet from the house, fracturing his skull. Their oldest child, twenty-one-year-old William, was not at the farm during the storm, but he arrived at the family property the next day to witness the wreckage for himself. In less than a day, three members of the Childs family were now gone.

The loss of the farm and three family members all at once were an especially cruel twist of fate for Bowie and Mollie Childs. Three years prior, lightning struck their hay barrack and burned out the building and much of their stored hay and straw. And less than four months prior, they had lost another family member: Mollie's father, Aden Allnutt.

Possibly as a result of the tornado, Mollie's siblings all agreed that she should inherit their father's farm. A property deed from 1930 states that without a will left behind, Aden died intestate, which left the Allnutt children and their spouses to decide that Mollie should be allowed ownership of not only his sixty-two acres but also all the buildings that came with it. According to the deed, she bought the property for just $10, equivalent to less than $200 in today's dollars.

The sad reality of the up-county tornado is that this was by far not the only area in the country to be hit by this cyclonic spree. The tragedies here occurred as a part of the much larger Rye Cove tornado outbreak, named after the place where the tornado caused the greatest loss of life. Several hours before the outbreak hit Montgomery County, a tornado shot through Rye Cove High School in southwest Virginia, killing twelve students and one teacher.

Montgomery County's only major recorded tornado tore through the county's northeastern portion and took the lives of four people. One *Evening*

*Star* report from 1929 estimated that the damage left by the storm cost the county at least $75,000 (equivalent to over $1.3 million today).

Remember, whenever there's a gust that starts to pick up in MoCo, don't get too alarmed if it blows off your hat or pushes you back a little. That mildly inconvenient swoosh of wind could be way, way worse.

## Chapter 16

# Villainous "Villa" Thompson Blows a Fuse

In 1920, the brutal, incendiary murders of the Bolton-Shipley family led to the last criminal execution in Montgomery County. So why, why does no one talk about this story today? That's what I've wondered out loud while combing through articles in the *Montgomery County Sentinel*, the *Washington Times* and the *Evening Star*, slowly peeling back layer after layer. Why haven't I seen a reenactment on Investigation Discovery? Why haven't I come across a true crime podcast covering the quadruple homicide?

There are a lot of moving parts that come together in the literally explosive case of the Waters' Mill murders in Germantown. There's love. There's jealousy. There's even politics. And after four innocent lives had been lost, one man would come to be known as the last man to hang in Montgomery County, Maryland.

The first, and arguably most dangerous, player in this case is Guy Vernon Thompson, known throughout the Germantown neighborhood as Vernon or Villa (pronounced *vee*-yuh). Thompson was the oldest of the four major players in this case, born on January 28, 1880, in Hyattstown. He was also the oldest of John "Buck" Buchanan and Catherine Andrews Thompson's eleven children.

You might think that leading a pack of eleven children might have given Thompson the opportunity to act as a role model. We don't know much about his early life, but if his actions as an adult are any indication of how he was as a child, Buck and Catherine must have had their hands full. That's aside from caring for ten other children, of course.

According to Villa's friends, he started showing signs of mental illness at the age of eighteen. He joined the military to fight in Cuba during the Spanish-American War of 1898. While there, he contracted an unspecified fever, leaving him in what a *Washington Times* article quoted as a "condition of irresponsibility." This somewhat vague term was used throughout the late nineteenth and early twentieth centuries to describe cases of alcoholic intoxication or mental illness.

Thompson was not big in stature, but he was surprisingly tough, likely stemming from his experience as a private in the U.S. Army. As one story goes, he was cut with a razor and attacked by a posse of six men. Although he was bleeding severely, he took out a revolver and shot away at the men until all of them fled.

In a disturbing turn of events, Thompson got married at thirty-three years old to our youngest main character in this story, Hester May Earp, who wrote on her marriage license that her age was twenty-one. The fact is, she was only thirteen. This pairing greatly disturbed her protective Uncle John, who tried to stop the wedding from happening. While the two ultimately succeeded in tying the knot, Thompson was furious that his new uncle-in-law had attempted to ruin his plans.

It is most probable that on August 21, 1913, Thompson approached the window of John Earp's home and threw a rock at it. The rock broke through the window and hit Earp on the head, knocking him unconscious. Even though there were, apparently, no other suspects in the case and Thompson had clear motive, a jury acquitted him of the charge of assault with intent to murder as Thompson simply stated that he didn't do it and no one saw him do it.

This, however, is by far not the biggest offense committed by the should-be-more-infamous Villa. Let's introduce major player no. 3, Hattie Shipley. Born in Loudoun County, Virginia, in 1892 as Hattie Estelle Tavenner, she was sent to the farm of John Carruthers as a child, where she worked as a servant. It appears her family did not have the means take care of her. Later, she moved across the Potomac River to the small village of Unity, Maryland, located northwest of Brookeville.

Whatever hardships Hattie faced as a child could not prepare her for being married to Douglass Shipley, her first husband. Douglass was a troubled man who abused Hattie. He aimed to destroy whatever she cared about just to spite her. After Douglass's behavior sent him to prison in 1916, Hattie attempted to marry another Unity man, fifty-eight-year-old Thomas Brown in 1918. However, when Brown attempted to obtain the marriage license, he was rejected because Hattie had not yet divorced her first husband. With the collapse of this relationship, Hattie and her baby daughter, Evelyn, moved to Germantown, where Hattie became the housekeeper of thirty-five-year-old James Bolton.

Last but not least, James "Jim" Bolton rounds out the four main characters in this tragedy. Bolton was a blacksmith and farmhand whose marriage had also failed, having divorced his ex-wife, Della. He lived in the miller's house on the property of Julian Waters: thus, Waters' Mill. His housekeeper Hattie and little Evelyn also lived in this tiny house in the country. Bolton took care of Hattie, and the two struck up a romantic relationship, even though Hattie had not yet divorced her husband, Douglass. Hattie found herself pregnant with Bolton's child, and she gave birth to their son, Harold, in May 1919. The affair progressed into 1920, when early that year, Hattie became pregnant with their second child.

The Bolton-Shipley family may have gotten to live out a bucolic fairytale experience in peace if it weren't for neighbors like Vernon Thompson. Thompson and Bolton hated each other. Thompson accused Bolton of trying to steal his wife, Hester, from him after seeing them "together" by the train tracks one day. Thompson warned him to keep away from his wife, but Bolton—less intimidated by him than, perhaps, some other neighbors—disregarded him as ridiculous.

November 2, 1920, was Election Day, a day that would mark a deadly mistake made by one of the men. Thompson worked that day as a local representative for the Republican Party, encouraging the community to vote for the eventual winner, Warren G. Harding. As the day wound down, he noticed that his neighbor and enemy, James Bolton, had not cast his vote yet. Seeing an opportunity to put Bolton in his place, he headed out to Bolton's cabin to ensure that he would vote for the Republican Party.

Bolton answered the door to Thompson, who proceeded to pressure him to come and vote for every Republican nominee on the ballot. Bolton responded that he was too busy and declined the invitation. Thompson pulled out a shotgun, threatening that Bolton had better come down to vote unless he wanted a "load of buckshot."

Reportedly, neighbors gave Thompson the nickname Villa because he reminded them of Mexican general Pancho Villa, who was allegedly afraid of nothing. What Bolton did next would prove that he could be just as bold. Bolton calmly picked up a nearby corn cutter and brought the instrument down onto Thompson's head. He then walked back into the house, grabbed his revolver and shot the unwelcome guest in the neck. Finally, as Thompson lay critically injured, Bolton picked up the phone and called Montgomery General Hospital, suggesting that they come take the fallen man to the hospital. Bolton spent a short time in jail before getting out on bond, while Thompson fumed and recovered in the hospital for several days.

As November rolled on, Thompson seethed with more and more hatred. A *Washington Times* article stated that after he had been shot, he looked up at both Bolton and Hattie, declaring, "You've got me now, you… But I'll get both of you." This hatred continued to bubble and fester after he left the hospital.

At around eleven o'clock at night on November 17, a few days after Thompson's release from the hospital, Hester noticed that her husband had left their house and disappeared into the night. A few hours later, he returned, got into bed and talked with his wife for a while, admitting that he was going to use a set of keys he had to go steal something from Waters' and Thrift's warehouse, and then he left once again. Hester was apparently not too fazed by her husband's late-night activities—until daylight came and the rest of the town discovered a shocking scene.

On the morning of November 18, 1920, the community of Germantown awoke to the horrific news that the small cabin with Bolton, Hattie and her two children in it had exploded at around four thirty in the morning. The blast was so powerful that people in Chevy Chase, over sixteen miles away, reported that their windows rattled. Hattie Shipley was badly bruised and battered from the explosion, but she managed to escape the destruction and get help.

A little after four o'clock in the morning, as Evelyn and Harold lay sleeping, Bolton and Hattie had woken up to their bulldog's frenzied barking. Both of them had a feeling that something was terribly wrong. Bolton went to grab his revolver but suddenly remembered that the police had confiscated the weapon because of the incident two weeks prior. As the dog continued to bark, Bolton feared investigating the trouble without his gun, so the dog and the two lovers continued their vigilant watch.

A few minutes later, Hattie finally felt herself falling asleep when— boom! The front of the house exploded, throwing people and belongings everywhere. Hattie was severely hurt but not as critically as Bolton, who was bleeding profusely from a head wound. Hattie recalled to the *Star* that he cried, "My God, my God, Hattie, do something for me, or I will bleed to death," as she tried to calm him down in case the attacker was still there. Hattie cautiously crossed the floor of the house to look for her children. She saw no sign of Harold, but by the light of a small fire, she saw Evelyn struggling to breathe under the weight of a beam that had fallen from the ceiling. She removed the beam from her daughter's neck and tucked a coat beneath her head to make her more comfortable.

As soon as she sensed the coast was clear, Hattie left the house in search of help. She crawled for half a mile through fields, over hills and across two frigid streams—remarkably, while she was eight months pregnant. More than an hour later, her weak cries reached the front door of her previous boss Slagle Dorsey and his family, who quickly took her in from the elements and summoned Sheriff George Nicholson to investigate the scene at Waters' Mill.

When the sheriff arrived on the scene, he discovered the dead bodies of three-year-old Evelyn Shipley and one-year-old Harold Shipley. Evelyn had died shortly after the explosion, and Harold had been killed instantly by falling debris. The sheriff found Bolton alive but unconscious and critically injured. Both adult victims were taken to Montgomery General.

It wasn't difficult to figure out who was responsible for the murders at Waters' Mill. All signs pointed to Vernon Thompson, who had spent time telling many of his neighbors the same thing he told Bolton and Hattie: that he was going to "get" Bolton. The *Times* reported that even Thompson's mother, Catherine, told him when she heard the news, "Well, I guess you will be arrested for this," to which he replied, "Yes, I guess I will."

Forensic evidence also pointed to Thompson's guilt. Fingerprints found at the crime scene matched Thompson's. At Waters' and Thrift's warehouse, where Thompson had told his wife he was going to steal some food, the warehouse reported theft of not food but a fifty-pound box of dynamite. Thompson's fingerprints were found at the warehouse, and close to a dozen dynamite caps were found lying around Bolton's home. Police also found footprints and dog tracks leading from Thompson's house over toward his enemy's property. In Thompson's house, police found several more dynamite caps.

As doctors treated Bolton and Hattie in the hospital, both victims accused Thompson of being the perpetrator. Hattie expressed that she could not understand how he could have done this terrible deed to her two babies. Bolton told the *Times*, "Thompson had threatened to get us and I suppose he has got me." These would be his last words.

For several hours, Bolton wavered in and out of consciousness at the hospital. Unlike his girlfriend, he had sustained a ruptured kidney and internal bleeding, and Dr. Jacob Bird's team fought a losing battle to save his life. He died less than a day after receiving his injuries, on the night of November 18, 1920, at the age of thirty-five. Meanwhile, Hattie's pain and suffering continued two days later when she had to deliver their son in her weakened state. While Hattie survived the birth—yet another harrowing experience—the baby was stillborn, likely killed in the blast and his body showing signs of the severe physical trauma he received due to Thompson's actions.

Three of the murder victims were buried in Rockville, while one was buried in Gaithersburg. Bolton was buried in Forest Oak Cemetery and shares a stone with his nephew, Willie Lowe. Since Hattie could not afford funerals for her three children, the towns of Germantown, Rockville and Gaithersburg banded together under the leadership of Sheriff Nicholson and a young woman named Minnie Yearley, who collected $150 from neighbors to help Hattie pay for her children's funeral costs. Because of Yearley's efforts, Evelyn, Harold and their baby brother share a marked gravestone in Rockville Cemetery to this day.

Hester and Vernon Thompson were quickly arrested on suspicion of the murders, but only Vernon was indicted, on the charge of first-degree murder. Hester ended up being a valuable witness in the trial against her

From the *Evening Star*, November 19, 1920: The center photo depicts Vernon Thompson (*standing, to the right*) as he is arrested for murder. The other photos show Jim Bolton's destroyed home. *Reprinted with permission of the DC Public Library, Star Collection © Washington Post.*

A newsboy holds up a copy of the *Washington Times* with the story of the dynamiting of the Bolton home on its front page, November 18, 1920. *LOC.*

husband. Initially, police hesitated to trust her judgment because she was allegedly illiterate and used a clock with only one hand on it to tell the time. However, she corroborated the police's suspicions that Thompson went out twice that night and admitted that she told him to hide his warehouse keys if anyone asked about them.

Faced with the mounting evidence against him, Thompson admitted that he broke into the warehouse that night but denied stealing anything. According to the *Star*, he claimed that he was looking for "grub" but did not find what he wanted, so he left. He consistently stated that he had nothing to do with the quadruple murders.

Frustrated, the police decided to try a new strategy to get Thompson to confess. Sheriff Nicholson took him out of jail on a field trip to see the bodies of the Shipley children and asked him if he knew them. Thompson looked them over calmly, and though he had been neighbors with the children, he claimed that he had never seen them before in his life.

When this failed to produce a confession, Nicholson brought him over to see Bolton's body. He asked Thompson if he murdered the man. Thompson hesitated, refusing to look over at the body, but Nicholson kept pressing him to look. As the *Times* reported, when he looked over at his old enemy, he did so with "burning hate." When Nicholson demanded again that he answer whether he killed Bolton or not, Thompson lost his temper. "What do you want me to do, kiss him?!" he snapped back at Nicholson. Annoyed and defeated, Nicholson and the authorities brought Thompson back to jail.

Although he insisted on his innocence, the name Vernon Thompson became synonymous with the murders. Newspapers across the country reported that Thompson was likely responsible for the killings. Coverage of the event spread from states like Arkansas to Connecticut, Florida to Oregon. Back home, on November 25, Governor Albert Ritchie of Maryland received a tip that a mob of fifty residents from Rockville and Germantown had made plans to raid the jail in Rockville where Thompson was being held to lynch him. Ritchie alerted Sheriff Nicholson, who hastily transferred Thompson from Rockville to Baltimore for his safety.

In early January 1921, the trial of Guy Vernon Thompson was held at the Montgomery County Circuit Court in Rockville. Thompson appeared indifferent as the state's attorney presented the case against him, while his own attorney made more of an effort to convince the jury not to sentence his client to death than to ask them to acquit him. Hester took the stand against her husband, saying that she still deeply loved him after the murders. Nonetheless, she testified that he had come home with the dynamite after all and that he had planned to use it to blow up Bolton's house. When Hattie took the stand and described the horrors she experienced in the explosion, Thompson continued to yawn and look bored with the whole procedure.

The jury only needed less than two and a half hours to come back with the verdict that Thompson was guilty of first-degree murder. Chief Judge Hammond Urner condemned the crime as "atrocious" and acknowledged that the jury had made the right decision. His punishment? Thompson would become the first Montgomery County man in two decades to face the hangman's noose.

Following his sentencing, Thompson was transferred back from Rockville to Baltimore. His attorney, John Garrett, tried his best to save him from the death penalty. Garrett tried to persuade Governor Ritchie to commute Thompson's sentence to life imprisonment or test Thompson for insanity, but the governor refused. In the weeks leading up to his scheduled day of execution, Thompson came to peace with his death. A March 1921 article in the *Times* related his fearlessness once again to that of the famed Pancho Villa, detailing his response when Sheriff Nicholson asked if Thompson would like anything from him: "No, Sheriff, there is nothing you can do for me but place the rope around my neck when the time comes. I will face death like a man. I am ready to meet my God."

The day when Thompson would meet his God finally came on April 15, 1921. At Thompson's request, Sheriff Nicholson postponed the execution until a few hours after sunrise so that he could say goodbye to visiting relatives and talk with his spiritual adviser. Then, at 9:36 a.m., about one hundred people watched as Nicholson sprung the trapdoor. Thompson had asked the sheriff if he could open up the jail yard and let even more people watch him hang, but Nicholson refused.

Eight minutes later, forty-one-year-old Villa's reign of terror officially came to an end. A crudely etched gravestone at Neelsville Presbyterian Church Cemetery in Germantown marks the final resting place of Thompson and his sister Blanche, who died fourteen years before him.

One odd coincidence seems to hang over this case. Vernon Thompson and James Bolton were mortal enemies, but they were also family. One of Vernon's brothers, Jesse Thompson, married Daisy Lowe, who was Bolton's niece. Hopefully, if they crossed paths at family reunions, Vernon and James managed to play nice for the time being. And in another strange turn of events, both parties are distantly related to me: Thompson is a third cousin three times removed, Bolton a third cousin four times removed. But I digress.

Twenty years to the month after Vernon Thompson was hanged for murder, his brother Dewey Thompson found himself in a similar situation. The Thompsons' family friends and former neighbors John and Clara Robertson came up to Germantown from Bethesda for a visit on the evening of April 27, 1941. Dewey and the Robertsons got into a drunken, violent argument over a charge of disorderly conduct brought against Dewey two weeks prior. Dewey ended up shooting both Robertsons, wounding John in the arm and Clara, fatally, in the heart. The trial would have taken place in Rockville, but Dewey's lawyers successfully petitioned for his trial to be moved to Leonardtown in St. Mary's County. With the new venue, he would have a better chance of receiving a fair and impartial trial without the outcome of the case being affected by his brother Vernon's legacy. Dewey Thompson was sentenced to life imprisonment for the first-degree murder of Clara Robertson and sent to the Maryland Penitentiary in Baltimore.

Following her husband's death, Hester's admission of love came into serious question because of what she did immediately afterward. Only five days had passed when on April 20, twenty-one-year-old Hester renounced her widowhood and was married to her second husband—by the same pastor who had attended Thompson right before his execution. In the seven years she was married to Thompson, the couple did not have any children. But over the course of the next twenty-five years with her new beau, Hester changed her name and became mother to their not one, not two, but fifteen children. She passed away in 1966.

It's amazing to think that Hattie, too, could move on after the sudden and traumatic deaths of her three children and her long-term romantic partner. It's even more striking when you consider that Evelyn, Harold and her baby boy weren't even the first of her children to be murdered.

September 15, 1916, was a fateful day for Hattie; her husband, Douglass; and their daughter, Sarah Elizabeth Shipley. Sarah had just celebrated her first birthday four days before, but the atmosphere at Shipleys' cottage at Unity was anything but festive. Although Douglass tended to be abusive and jealous toward his wife, on this day, he chose to redirect his anger at the child he knew she loved so much. I would rather tell you the basics and spare you the more gruesome details of this case, because this is a heartbreaking story. If you really want to read more about it, I suggest looking at page 10 of the September 17, 1916 edition of the *Evening Star*.

In short, Douglass said he wanted to "get even with" Hattie, so he physically tortured Sarah for an entire day. Hattie attempted to save her daughter, but when she tried to interfere, Douglass threatened to kill her too. Once the ordeal had ended, Hattie fled the house in an eerily similar fashion to what would happen four years later. She ran across a field and through the woods to her neighbor Artemus Griffith's house. This time, she was running while pregnant with her daughter, Evelyn. Hattie called the police to summon them to her house, but when they arrived at the Shipley cottage, they discovered they were too late to save Sarah's life.

At twenty-four years old, Douglass Shipley was charged with the first-degree murder of his daughter. Coincidentally, Shipley was represented by the same lawyer who would represent Thompson, John Garrett. Garrett used a similar strategy in both cases, trying to make the point that his client deserved a less severe sentence because he might suffer from insanity. While Thompson would receive the death penalty, Shipley avoided the noose and was sentenced to life imprisonment at the Maryland Penitentiary in Baltimore, where he died in 1944 at the age of fifty-two.

After an abusive marriage, the murders of four children and the loss of the man who did love and care for her and her children, what did Hattie do next? After five years of being married to a husband in prison, Hattie finally got the funds she needed to divorce him. She remarried, to Charles Maraskey, within a couple years of the Waters' Mill tragedy and had four more children, all of whom lived into adulthood. She continued to be a housekeeper after moving to Ellicott City, Maryland, where she died in 1953 at the age of sixty.

The turmoil in Hattie's life did slow down—but not completely. While living in Laytonsville in 1925, she was arrested and sentenced to six months in prison for keeping a "disorderly house," a term that commonly referred to an illegal brothel or casino. In her later years, Hattie evidently hid the details of her past from her family. Her granddaughter Betty Huber recalls hearing nothing about her tragic backstory until decades later, when her son Lee got curious and did some family research. In another shocking twist, yet another one of Hattie's children met a tragic end after her death. In 1972, her forty-three-year-old son Willard Maraskey was swept away and drowned in his car when Hurricane Agnes flooded the streets of Ellicott City.

After moving away from Montgomery County, Hattie Shipley-Maraskey (*pictured*) seemingly never discussed the tragedies she had faced there. Her granddaughter Betty remembers Hattie as a very sweet woman who cared greatly for her as a child. *Betty and Lee Huber.*

Since Thompson, there have been no executions in Montgomery County. Execution by hanging in the state of Maryland became history in 1955 when the state legislature changed its preferred method to the gas chamber. In 1994, it was changed again to lethal injection, and in 2013, capital punishment was completely abolished in the state. However, if you visit the Montgomery County Historical Society in Rockville, the morbidly curious can view part of the original rope used to make the noose in Thompson's hanging.

The ruins of the Waters' miller's house, the scene of the Bolton-Shipley murders, lie at the corner of the Hard Rock Trail and Lake Ridge Drive in Black Hill Regional Park near Germantown. Families bike down the path in the summer past one of Montgomery County's most well-hidden crime scenes. Less than a mile away, at the ruins of Waters' Mill, a plaque details the ownership and usage of the mill but makes no mention of the disturbing history between Villa Thompson and Jim Bolton. When you consider the fact that parents and their little kids pass by this place every day for several months out of the year, is it really that surprising?

## Chapter 17

# ASPIN HILL PET (AND HUMAN) CEMETERY

Jamie Albanesi was a little guy with a big gravestone. Passing his plot, I walked up, saw a huge heart with the name "Jamie" inscribed on it and immediately thought, *Wow, this kid was only fourteen when he passed.* And then I looked again and saw it. On the gravestone, there was a picture of Jamie, clearly a Pomeranian, regally posing and sticking out his tongue.

Looking around Aspin Hill Pet Cemetery, also known as Aspin Hill Memorial Park, forces you to realize how devoted humans can be to their animals. Many of the stones are at least two to three feet tall and feature moving epitaphs in honor of beloved pets.

For instance, you may not know much about Sonny Boy Rosen, who looks to be a Cavalier King Charles Spaniel by his picture and whose stone indicates he lived from October 1949 to February 1956. You don't know what he did, you don't know what his bark sounded like, but you can tell how he made his owners feel from the message inscribed on his gravestone:

*My pal*
*Who possessed beauty without vanity*
*Strength without insolence*
*Courage without ferocity*
*And all the virtues of man*
*Without his vices this praise*
*Is but a just tribute to the memory of Sonny Boy.*
*Part of my heart is buried here.*

Tucked behind a grove of trees at the corner of Aspen Hill Road and Georgia Avenue, *Aspin* Hill is the fifth oldest continuously operating pet cemetery in the United States. In July 1920, Richard and Bertha Birney bought about ten acres of land, where they planned to breed dogs, run a boarding kennel and start a pet cemetery. While the community of Aspen Hill was named for the aspen trees that grew in the area, the Aspin Hill property may have been named after a famous English kennel of the same name and spelling.

Thanks to the hard work of cemetery historian Julianne Mangin, Aspin Hill's rich past has been thoroughly uncovered. According to her research with the American Humane Society, the first burial in the cemetery was the interment of a St. Bernard. Since then, over fifty thousand pets have been buried here as well as around fifty-five owners who just couldn't stand to be too far apart from their beloved companions, even in the afterlife.

According to Mangin, the pet cemetery grew in the 1920s to over 1,400 interments, a number that wholly surprised Richard and Bertha. The Birneys encouraged the extravagant, gushy epitaphs and dramatic mourning rituals that some pet owners decided to enact at their pets' graves. Richard said in a 1925 interview with the *Evening Star*, "To me in this work-a-day, selfish world, those stones there tell a beautiful story. Maybe we all aren't as jazz-crazed and pleasure-mad as some people would have us believe."

One of the earliest and most frequent visitors to the cemetery was Mrs. Selma Snook, the wife of a deputy marshal in Washington, D.C. Snook adored her pets, which were mainly French poodles. In the 1920s, she buried at least five dogs—Boots, Buster, Snowball, Trixie and Little Jeff—and one cat, Blackie, at the cemetery. If you had seen any of these proceedings, you might have thought that the president had died.

When it came to her little ones, Mrs. Snook knew how to set up a funeral like no one else would. On July 8, 1922, her fourteen-year-old Havanese dog, Snowball, died of old age on the satin pillow he had slept on for the past five years. Three days later, friends, both human and dog, gathered in the Snooks' home in Columbia Heights to say goodbye to their pal, Snowball. The following 1922 article from the *Alexandria Gazette* elaborates: "The 'body' was laid out in the parlor and the tiny white casket was covered by a pillow of red and white roses, with a large white snowball in the centre. There the mourners paid their silent tribute to the departed doggie."

Once the wake was finished, four neighborhood boys acted as pallbearers. Three of Snowball's friends, an English setter and two French bulldogs, guarded them as they escorted Snowball, his family and friends to the

Selma Snook buries her Spanish poodle, Buster, at Aspin Hill Cemetery, 1921. *LOC.*

gravesite. Mrs. Snook tearfully paid her final respects and sent up a quiet prayer for her dear pooch.

Many dogs like Snowball received elaborate send-offs here after their deaths. One Boston terrier, Mickey, even has his own mausoleum. And it's not just dogs and cats. Pet birds, horses, turtles and snakes rest in peace here, too. The cemetery is also notable for its plaques mourning animal cruelty, such as one for "Emily, Jane, Annie, Rue, and the millions of rats used in medical experimentation and product testing." Another stone, picturing a raccoon and a mink, states: "Hundreds of defenseless animals suffered and died to be made into the coats that lie here. Products of human ignorance and vanity."

While the cemetery has held a special place in the hearts of many animal owners, it has not always welcomed every animal with pleasure. In a 1946 piece from his column in the *Chicago Defender*, Adventures in Race Relations, Black writer Alfred E. Smith told the story of Roy A. Ellis, a Black man who worked for the U.S. Department of Labor. Ellis had wanted

*Left*: The final resting place of Betty Slaton and her beloved Phobie. *Author's collection.*

*Below*: The Lab Rat memorial. *Author's collection.*

*Opposite, left*: Jamie Albanesi's grave. *Author's collection.*

*Opposite, right*: Mickey the dog's mausoleum. *Author's collection.*

to bury his precious spitz dog in the cemetery. The cemetery's response? "Aspin Hill does not bury colored dogs." The irony of the situation? Ellis's dog was white.

In the years since its opening, several notable pets have received burials at Aspin Hill. FBI director J. Edgar Hoover buried seven dogs in the cemetery. When the lawman wasn't tracking down gangsters or communists, it turned out, he was just playing with his terriers. There's also Rags, a famous mascot and messenger dog during World War I; Timmie, a cat known for his unusual bond with Calvin Coolidge's canary; and Mack, a Seeing Eye dog well-known in his hometown of Alexandria, Virginia.

Of course, there's also Napoleon the white Persian cat, who became famous in Baltimore for his "weather forecasts." His owner, Fannie DeShields, claimed that whenever he slept on his stomach rather than his side, there would be a change of weather within twenty-four hours. When the City of Baltimore realized that these predictions were relatively accurate, Napoleon gained the title of "Weather Prophet of Baltimore," which is inscribed on his gravestone to this day.

Aspin Hill Pet Cemetery has changed hands between several families and organizations over the past century. The Montgomery County Humane Society currently owns the property but, according to Mangin, it is not offering any more burial plots at this time because the previous owners, the Chesapeake Wildlife Society, did not leave behind any sales records. Since the humane society has no way of knowing whether an empty plot has been sold or not, they cannot sell any more until the records may become available.

In recent years, the cemetery has become disheveled. You have to watch your step in the tall grass for holes, sunken patches and a crushed-up beer can or two. The humane society plans to build a new headquarters on the adjacent property, where the Birneys used to live. The development would include a veterinary clinic, an administrative office, an adoption center and a revitalization of the cemetery, but from Mangin's understanding, the process could take years.

Putting the current hazards aside, visiting Aspin Hill is a beautiful experience. Reading the cutesy names and long, saccharine inscriptions can make you reconsider this place of the dead as one big celebration of life, to which our pets bring joy and meaning every day.

PART IV

# ENTERTAINMENT

# Chapter 18

# AN AMUSING HISTORY OF GLEN ECHO PARK

Back in elementary school, my class took a field trip to the Clara Barton House, a rite of passage for many a kid living in Montgomery County. After a tour of the American Red Cross founder's home, we ran next door to what we had been told was an amusement park.

It *was* an amusement park. There was a carousel, yes, and a playground, but I wondered: *What happened to the rest of the rides?* Turns out, we all got there forty years too late.

Twin brothers Edwin and Edward Baltzley founded the town of Glen Echo in 1888 and the National Chautauqua of Glen Echo in 1891. Using the money from an eggbeater design Edwin had patented, the brothers decided to develop a new resort community on the Potomac River. At the center, a five-story hotel and restaurant called the Patawomeck Café offered guests breathtaking views of the Potomac River from its balconies.

During its brief history, the National Chautauqua of Glen Echo had become a center for both biblical seminars and general leisure. The Baltzley brothers recruited the famous humanitarian Clara Barton as a sponsor for the Chautauqua settlement. To sweeten the deal, in 1891, they built Barton her very own house, the one that stands in Glen Echo today and that would become the headquarters for the American Red Cross in 1897.

Luck was not on the Baltzleys' side. The Patawomeck Café burned down just six months after opening. In yet another tragic event, rumors of malaria spreading from Glen Echo to Washington, D.C., caused vacationers to flee the resort town. By 1893, the Chautauqua meetings were no more. The Baltzley brothers plunged into debt and eventually abandoned Glen Echo.

Affectionately nicknamed the Air Castle, Patawomeck Café looks out over the Potomac River. Six months after opening in 1891, it burned down in a fire. *MCHS.*

With the extension of the Washington and Great Falls trolley line from Georgetown to Glen Echo in 1896, electricity came to town. The park's new investors decided to utilize this resource to build an amusement park that included attractions like a carousel, a ride called the Gyroplane and a roller coaster called the Dip.

In 1906, Lorenzo Shaw became the new manager of Glen Echo Park, and he wanted more, more and more. Unlike the Baltzley brothers, Shaw did not get along well with beloved local Clara Barton. He asked her to let him turn her house into a hotel for the park. She said no.

The endeavor could have ended there without escalating, but it didn't. You see, Shaw resorted to pettiness when he didn't get his way, and whether or not Barton was an eighty-four-year-old national treasure, he felt she needed to cooperate. Historian Richard Cook recounts that first, Shaw tried to use a legal loophole in the original deed to her house to force her out, but that didn't work. Then he built a "scenic railway" ride around her house and plopped a Ferris wheel right in her front yard. Finally, he restructured the Dip so that the coaster went right by one of her windows.

Barton knew he was trying to force her out, but she didn't care. Seemingly unfazed by her updated surroundings, she wrote in her diary one summer night in 1906: "The evenings are very pretty—the lights cheerful. The noise in no way disturbs us."

Ironically, in 1908, Shaw found himself in deep financial trouble with the park and asked Barton to loan him money. After years of harassment, she, of course, said no. Barton had finally defeated Shaw and lived out the rest of her life in peace. She died in 1912, a few months after her ninetieth birthday. In case you haven't seen her house lately, all the amusement park rides have since been removed from her lawn.

In 1911, the Washington Railway and Electric Company became the new managers of Glen Echo Park, with Leonard Schloss now head of operations. Thanks to Schloss's leadership, the park became one of the most popular amusement parks around Washington. The year 1921 saw a new roller coaster called Coaster Dips become the park's main attraction, along with a brand-new Dentzel carousel. Riders could enjoy this unique carousel fitted with not just horses but also rabbits, ostriches and many other animals.

During the 1920s, attendance at the park commonly reached over ten thousand people per weekend. The caterpillar ride, Midway funhouse, Skooter bumper cars and a ride called the Flying Skooter made up just a few of its whimsical attractions. The park's Crystal Pool became a popular public pool for Montgomery Countians. Summer visitors could splash, slide and dive in the water or relax on a beach of imported sand if they preferred. The island in the middle of the pool would even serve as a stage for concerts from time to time.

When they weren't lining up for rides, visitors could socialize, swing dance or enjoy a show at the Spanish Garden Ballroom, the main performance venue at the park. Built in 1933, the ballroom hosted acts like Howdy Doody, Lawrence Welk and Bill Haley & His Comets over the next few decades. Before his turn as a beloved *Today Show* weatherman, Willard Scott came to Glen Echo Park as a child and later performed his Bozo the Clown act here.

Two of the most popular rides at the park have been the setting for four accidental deaths at Glen Echo Park. In 1918, Joseph Hammell fell from the scenic railway and died. Three years later, in 1921, park employee James Shanholtz was also killed falling off one of the railway cars.

Three more years passed, and in 1924, another man, Thomas Monohan, fell to his death at the park. While riding the Coaster Dips, Monahan decided to stand up—but lost his balance and then his life. Yet another man named William Lawrence was killed when he fell off the same ride in 1929.

There is, however, one alleged death that the park has refuted. During the summer of 1940, a rumor spread that on its "tunnel of love" ride called the World Cruise, a girl died because she was bit by a venomous snake. There was no evidence to prove this claim; nonetheless, the hoax caused so much public panic that Leonard Schloss got the police involved to find whoever initiated the slander against his park. He also placed an ad in the Washington papers disclaiming the rumor and asking for information that might lead to the culprit's arrest.

One reporter named Thomas R. Henry pointed out in a July 24, 1940 article for the *Evening Star* that the story bore a certain resemblance to an old urban legend. There was always a girl, there was always some fantastic story about how she suddenly died and the storyteller always heard the story from some ridiculously distant source, like "a niece of [a] divorced wife's sister-in-law."

The summer of 1960 was another turbulent season for Glen Echo Park. Civil rights activists from the Non-Violent Action Group (NAG) came to protest the park's long history of segregation. Around two dozen students, both Black and White, many from Howard University, demanded that they all be able to enter the park together. Residents of the Bannockburn neighborhood in nearby Bethesda witnessed the NAG's protests and were inspired to join them on the picket lines. The majority of Bannockburn's residents were either White or Jewish.

"The Beach" of imported sand at Glen Echo Park, circa 1935. Nearly five hundred people are enjoying the pool in the upper left of the picture. *MCHS.*

A young man pickets outside Glen Echo Park during the Bannockburn civil rights protest, 1960. *MCHS.*

The long line going into Glen Echo Park's Coaster Dips rollercoaster. Coaster Dips was known as the park's most popular attraction. *MCHS.*

While these demonstrations were mostly peaceful, they led to the arrest of five NAG protesters and counterprotests by George Lincoln Rockwell and the American Nazi Party. Bannockburn resident and assistant to the Secretary of Commerce Hyman Bookbinder escalated the issue to U.S. Secretary of State Robert F. Kennedy. Determined to help the NAG activists, Kennedy threatened to take the trolley away from Glen Echo Park if they refused to desegregate. The park finally relented, officially desegregating on March 14, 1961.

The amusement park would remain open for only another seven years, closing in 1968. People had become more mobile and stopped relying on the trolley for transportation. Instead, they were driving or flying to newer amusement parks like Disneyland. Glen Echo Park had suffered severe losses in profit, and reports of an alleged race riot there in 1966 tarnished its reputation.

In 1970, the park's acquisition by the National Park Service saved many of its remaining structures from residential development. Ten years later, in

1980, the park was added to the National Register of Historic Places. Today, Glen Echo Park is no longer an amusement park, but it acts as a center for arts and culture, offering lessons in subjects like theater, painting and glassblowing. Dance classes are offered in the still-existing Spanish Ballroom and bumper car pavilion. And while most of the rides no longer stand, the Dentzel carousel has been restored and still operates in the park.

## Chapter 19

# SEE THE FOREST FOR THE TREES—AND WASHINGTON GROVE, TOO

Hidden in plain sight and frozen in a Victorian setting, the town of Washington Grove lies in a forest on the eastern edge of Gaithersburg. Once upon a time, this land was settled as a Methodist summer camp, a spot for Christian adults to find fellowship and for their children to learn more about the Bible. This is the story of how one town sprouted from 258 tents.

In 1873, when United Methodist organizers from Washington, D.C., came upon Nathan Cooke's farm, they were excited to see hundreds of acres of woods along with plenty of drinking water flowing from Whetstone Branch. They purchased almost two hundred acres of the farmland and built up their permanent summer community along the tracks of the brand-new Metropolitan Branch of the B&O Railroad. The Methodists invested in features like wells, outhouses, sheds and tents to cater to visiting members and start their nonprofit corporation, the Washington Grove Association, off on the right track.

As the Metropolitan Branch grew in popularity, so did the Grove. According to Philip K. Edwards's book *Washington Grove: 1873–1937*, close to ten thousand people attended each camp meeting in the 1870s, and two hundred people converted to Methodism in the first two years.

The town grew around the "Sacred Circle," an area where men and women met to sing, eat, pray and exchange goods while their children played and attended Sunday school. These Chautauqua assemblies, as they were called, were popular in the late nineteenth and early twentieth centuries as a fun way for Christians of all ages to spread the Gospel while enjoying festive socialization, musicians and guest lecturers.

This was no ordinary summer camp. The Grove soon gained a barbershop, a hotel, a furniture store, a grocery store and an assembly hall. The assembly hall became not only a place for Methodist leaders to preach to campers but also a place for stockholders of the Washington Grove Association to meet. Between 1873 and 1937, investors would buy shares in the town to own tents—and, later, cottages for themselves, once they could afford more shares.

At the turn of the twentieth century, the Grove made a clear effort to become more relaxed. In the 1900s, the Grove added a baseball diamond and tennis courts. Along came a man-made swimming hole, Maple Lake, in 1910, electricity in 1914 and full telephone coverage in 1920. The community even decided to drop the "Camp Meeting" part of its name to officially become Washington Grove in 1906. In 1915, Washington Grove hosted its first movie night at the assembly hall, now known as McCathran Hall. The controversial *Birth of a Nation* was the first movie shown there.

With all these amenities abounding, many of the Grove's summer visitors decided to become permanent, year-round residents during the 1920s. As

RAILROAD STATION, Washington Grove, Md.

Postcard from Connie Mullinix to her mother, Clara, depicting the railroad station at Washington Grove, circa 1920. Connie writes about a recent trip to Georgetown. *MCHS.*

The Assembly Hall and Hotel at Washington Grove, circa 1909. *MCHS.*

Maple Lake, 1955. For over a century, Maple Lake has been the central swimming spot for Washington Grove residents and their guests. *MCHS.*

the community began looking more like a resort town, the need for local government became more pressing. The suggestion was made for Washington Grove to merge with Gaithersburg in 1930, but by 1937, Washington Grove had proved it could hold its own. That year, it was officially incorporated as the Town of Washington Grove. The shares became lots and deeds, and the Grove's camp meeting structure evolved into a mayor and town council.

Since its incorporation in 1937, Washington Grove has continued to draw curious city folk to its bucolic setting. In the 1940s and '50s, it served as a bedroom community for U.S. government workers, who could walk to the nearby train station and commute to Washington, D.C. The town has valiantly fought against developers and now stresses preservation. In the 1950s, it witnessed the nearby historically Black community of Emory Grove disappear to make way for a new residential projects. New neighborhoods and roads have continued to creep up around Washington Grove, but it remains the "Town within a Forest," as its motto says.

In 1980, Washington Grove was added to the National Register of Historic Places. Many original buildings like the hotel and the furniture store are gone, but the residents of Washington Grove still find time to eat, laugh and sing at picnics and concerts held at their own Woodward Park and McCathran Hall.

Although it has been replaced and repaired many times since the 1870s, a steep railroad bridge called the Humpback Bridge from the town's early history still survives. In 2009, it was added to the National Register of Historic Places. This overpass holds the distinction of being the only surviving bridge in Montgomery County built over the Metropolitan Branch by the B&O Railroad.

Chapter 20

# Ladies and Gentlemen, the Cornet Band

Long before the days of Lynyrd Skynyrd and the Jonas Brothers, the residents of Montgomery County jammed out to the cornet bands that played throughout their communities. During the late nineteenth and early twentieth centuries, when options for leisure activity were limited, many farmers and tradesmen found a convenient pastime in gathering together to play music.

Although they were called "cornet bands," a number of different instruments were played in each band. Of course, some early band members played the cornet, but they were accompanied by other brass instruments like the baritone, bass horn and trombone. Other instruments included the piccolo, saxophone and clarinet. Bands from King's Valley, Browningsville and Potomac had their names printed on the heads of their bass drums.

Two of the first of these bands were from Poolesville and Clarksburg, followed by a burst of new local bands during the 1880s and '90s. From Washington Grove to Brookeville to Travilah, the men of these communities now had an outlet to express their musical talent at local parades, carnivals, church picnics, Fourth of July festivals and more.

At only seventeen years old, William Walker started the Browningsville Community Cornet Band on the outskirts of Damascus. His father, George Walker, inspired his decision to pursue performing. George Walker taught music and led a choir in the area for several years, gaining the nickname Professor Walker from his community. In the nineteenth century, *professor* was a title loosely given to music teachers and band leaders regardless of their educational background.

*Left*: William A. Walker, who founded the Browningsville Band in 1884 at the age of seventeen. *Browningsville Band.*

*Right*: James S. Day, cofounder of the Browningsville Band, in his uniform in 1890. *Browningsville Band.*

The Browningsville Band is the only continuously operating cornet band left from its era in Montgomery County. Band member Elise George writes that the band first came together on a chilly day in January 1884. Across the surrounding farmlands, twenty boys and men from the ages of eleven to twenty-nine trudged to the paint shop of Jonathan Jacobs in Browningsville to play for the first time together.

Walker, Moxley, Watkins, Mullinix and Day: these are just some of the family names passed from generation to generation through the evolving rosters of the Browningsville Band. James Start Day was eighteen years old when he became a founding member of the band. He couldn't have known it at the time, but both his son Raymond and his grandson Basil would be its directors someday.

Day's great-granddaughter and William Walker's great-grandniece Merhlyn Barnes also became members of the band. In a 2011 episode of *Paths to the Present: Montgomery County Stories*, Barnes demonstrated her skill with the glockenspiel, an instrument she had played in the band since

*This page, top*: The Stringtown Band, a precursor to the King's Valley Band, circa 1875. *MCHS.*

*This page, bottom*: The Browningsville Cornet Band, 1890. *Browningsville Band.*

*Opposite*: The King's Valley Band, circa 1900. *MCHS.*

she was twelve years old. She joined in the 1950s, one of the first female members of the band.

Over 140 years, from the marches of John Philip Sousa to the eras of Taylor Swift, the Browningsville Band has survived. The times may have changed, but the band's passion for playing music remains the same.

Chapter 21

# The Star-Studded Shady Grove Music Fair

Did you grow up in MoCo during the 1960s and '70s? Chances are you remember those days when instead of heading over to Merriweather Post Pavilion or Jiffy Lube Live to see your favorite performers, the best venue was much closer to home. For fifteen years, the Shady Grove Music Fair in Gaithersburg offered county residents the chance to see plays, concerts and comedians without a lengthy drive.

The Shady Grove Music Fair lay on twelve acres previously owned by real estate developer Sam Eig (sound familiar?). The property was located at the intersection of Shady Grove Road and I-70S (now I-270), a mile down the road from what is now Sam Eig Highway. Concert promoters and business partners Shelly Gross, Lee Guber and Frank Ford began work on the property by building a large circular tent that would accommodate 2,200 eventgoers. One of the venue's developers, Lee Guber, went on to marry a woman who had started writing for the *Today* show in the early 1960s. The woman's name was Barbara Walters, and she would remain his wife from 1963 until their divorce in 1976.

After much excitement and buildup, the Music Fair opened on June 18, 1962, with an 8:30 p.m. staging of the musical *Brigadoon*, starring Dorothy Collins and Stanley Grover. The weeklong show was a monumental success, especially thanks to the efforts of Attorney General Robert F. "Bobby" Kennedy and his wife, Ethel. Bobby and Ethel sponsored a benefit performance of *Brigadoon* on the afternoon of June 20. The couple came up from Washington along with their family and two thousand underprivileged area children to see the show under the tent in Gaithersburg.

Actress Marlo Thomas (*left*) and Lynda Bird Johnson (*right*), daughter of President Lyndon B. Johnson, attend a performance at the Music Fair, early 1960s. *MCHS.*

Over the years, the Shady Grove Music Fair had its fair share of big names come to entertain locals. Legendary singers like Ray Charles, Dionne Warwick and Tony Bennett came to perform in Gaithersburg, as did comedians like Don Rickles, Redd Foxx and Johnny Carson. Then there were stars like Ella Fitzgerald, the Steve Miller Band, Lily Tomlin, James Brown—the list goes on and on. Olympic champion figure skater Peggy Fleming performed twice at the Music Fair, once in 1972 and again in 1973.

The Music Fair grew to be a focus for the community of Montgomery County. A permanent structure that would hold five thousand people replaced the tent in 1967 and became the venue for many Montgomery County high school graduations. While in recent history, many MoCo high schoolers have graduated at DAR Constitution Hall in Washington, the Shady Grove Music Fair was once the place to get your diploma and a round of applause.

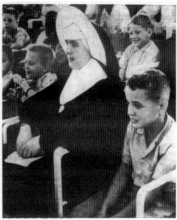

**'BRIGADOON' MAKES BOW FOR CHILDREN**

Occasional rain fell on a soggy plain near Gaithersburg, Md., yesterday where 2,000 underprivileged children from the Washington area saw a performance of Lerner and Loewe's "Brigadoon" as guests of the new Shady Grove Music Fair under the sponsorship of Attorney General and

Mrs. Robert Kennedy. A vending company distributed free hot dogs and cokes, here being enjoyed by Mrs. Kennedy, her son David, Alice Ormsby Gore, daughter of British Ambassador and Lady Ormsby Gore, and Kathleen Kennedy under the shelter of a tent.

Sister Marian Anthony watches the musical play "Brigadoon," with some of the children from St. Joseph's Home and School. Twenty-four buses and many automobiles transported the children to the special showing at the new summer theater-in-the-round. The stage is sheltered by a huge circus-type tent, fine for rainy days.—Star Staff Photos.

*Top left photo, left to right*: Ethel Kennedy, her son David, family friend Alice Ormsby-Gore and Ethel's daughter Kathleen enjoy refreshments at a Music Fair showing of Brigadoon. From the *Evening Star*, June 21, 1962. *Reprinted with permission of the DC Public Library, Star Collection © Washington Post.*

As the 1970s came around, the Shady Grove Music Fair struggled against local competition. Both the Kennedy Center and the Wolf Trap Farm Park (now National Park) for the Performing Arts opened in the area in 1971 and thrived as nonprofit organizations, taking away valuable customers and income from the Music Fair. Management tried to rebound by adding flashy lights to the roof of the dome so that they could draw the attention of passing cars on I-270. They also tried to promote more popular TV entertainers like Joan Rivers, Freddie Prinze and George Carlin, but their losses became irreversible and closure grew imminent. Some of the Music Fair's last events in 1977 included concerts by Tina Turner and Sonny and Cher, as well as performances of *Camelot* and *The Merry Widow*.

Following its closure, developers discussed turning the site into a luxury hotel or a shopping center. Ultimately, a complex of office buildings now stands in place of the Shady Grove Music Fair. Baby boomers might remember this plot of land for the wonderful times they had becoming more cultured and witnessing their favorite celebrities perform. If you were born after the Gerald Ford administration like me, then congratulations: you just gained a tad more appreciation for the history behind the tan corporate buildings down the road from Fallsgrove.

## Chapter 22

# BILLY AND PORKY, THE TRASH-TALKING ANIMALS

Porky had a brother! Or a cousin! Or whatever you would call the relationship between two disembodied animals who teach kids about the importance of throwing out their trash!

If you grew up going to Cabin John Regional Park, Porky the Litter-Eating Pig always either made your day or scared you to death. To this day, by pressing a button on the small brick house Porky calls home, you can bring him to life in the recording that plays. Squeaking and squealing and snorting, Porky jollily introduces himself to you:

> *Hi kids, I'm Porky the Litter Eater, and I sure like to eat. You can find me paper and cardboard and soft drink cans, but never, never feed me bottles or broken glass. Glass gives me a stomachache. Find me some paper now and watch me gobble it up. I'm hungry… hungry… hungry…*

The environmentally friendly Porky came to Cabin John in 1966, one year after his older "brother" Billy the Litter Eater came to Wheaton Regional Park. A caretaker at Wheaton Park, Ted Gurney, provided the voice of Porky. Press the button at Cabin John, and you'll still hear Gurney's voice almost sixty years later.

Billy the aptly named goat also lived in a tiny brick house and implored children to feed him garbage. Porky and Billy served to keep the park clean and litter-free so that both parks maintained a sparkling reputation. While Billy has been gone from Wheaton for a few decades now, Porky remains

*"Billy, the Little Eater" proved to be one of the most popular attractions at Wheaton Regional Park this year. Completed in early spring, "Billy" has a voracious appetite for all sorts of litter save broken glass—an appetite given strong support by a vacuum pump!*

at Cabin John Park to suck down any loose garbage through his vacuum-powered mouth. Don't worry, though. He only eats litter, not human appendages.

In the 1960s, these talkative paper-eating animals weren't just in Montgomery County; they were all over the country. New Orleans amusement park Pontchartrain Beach had some of the first vacuum-operated trash cans known as Porky the *Paper* Eater. A few years before Cabin John's Porky came into existence, there was the Pontchartrain Porky, who bore a swinish resemblance to the one at Cabin John but resided in a mushroom rather than a brick house. Did I miss the part where one of the three little pigs lived in a fungus?

As it turns out, the mushroom Porky was a popular fixture of Pontchartrain Beach before the park's closure in 1983. Other paper-eating variations included Pepe the Clown and Leo the Lion. Leo seemed to resonate more with kids than Pepe, as more Leos popped up at parks in Ohio, Pennsylvania and Ontario, too.

Rather than sandwiching a plea to keep the park clean between snorts, like Porky, Leo lets out a mighty roar from his cage. At the Lincoln Children's Zoo in Nebraska, Leo cheerfully reassures guests, "Oh, don't be scared; the only thing I eat is paper!" He goes on to tell them that while they can feed him paper, they should not feed the other animals at the zoo because "they all have very special diets."

Over the past six decades, the number of these "paper eaters" dwindled as amusement parks closed and government officials changed their priorities, but our Porky at Cabin John Park has survived. This was no easy feat for the little environmentalist. Wheaton and Cabin John Parks have both gone through major developments since opening in 1960 and 1966, respectively. Wheaton Regional Park started with a small nature center in the early 1960s but has expanded its attractions significantly to include Brookside Gardens, a carousel and an ice rink the size of those in the National Hockey League.

One of the attractions that did not survive was Old MacDonald's Farm, a petting zoo at Wheaton Park that First Lady Jackie Kennedy once visited

*Opposite*: Children feed Billy the Litter Eater at Wheaton Regional Park, 1965. *M-NCPPC.*

*Above*: Porky the Litter Eater has made his home at Cabin John Regional Park since 1966. *Author's collection.*

with her son John Jr. when he was a kid. After a few decades, the petting zoo closed, and Billy the Litter Eater went away with it. Cabin John also had a petting zoo called Noah's Ark long ago; a dog park now stands in its place.

When you think about it, it's not just that Porky and Billy were like brothers: the Wheaton and Cabin John Parks were, too. Both have kept similar attractions like an ice rink and a choo-choo train around for years. At one point, each park had a fighter jet on display from the Korean War era for kids to climb on and use like a playground.

Another quirky staple of Cabin John Park is its totem pole, which has stood on the grounds since 1966, like Porky. A 2022 article by Liz Ruskin for Alaska Public Media revealed that the totem pole was carved by members of the Tlingít tribe in Haines, Alaska. The pole was commissioned on behalf of the Potomac Area Council of Camp Fire Girls and then sent thousands of miles to its home in Bethesda.

One of the quirkiest things that Billy may have witnessed during his last years at Wheaton Regional Park was the squirrel attacks of 1990. In October that year, the playground there had to close temporarily when its squirrels became uncharacteristically aggressive toward humans, jumping at visitors, stealing their food and chomping on anyone who got in the way of their next meal. It sounds like an animated family comedy from DreamWorks, but it was actually pretty scary for some.

Howard Schneider retold the event in his *Washington Post* article "Crazed Critters Take Over Wheaton Park; Hungry Squirrels Become Over-Aggressive, Start Biting the Hands That Feed Them." Reportedly, the squirrels bit two children, and one man had to fight a bloody battle against one with a stick. Park employees believed that an unusually productive acorn harvest over the last two years had led to an increase in the local squirrel population. When visitors offered the squirrels some of their food, some squirrels got greedy and lunged at them, demanding more. Yellow tape surrounded the playground like a crime scene until park management felt people could safely visit without fear of squirrelly behavior.

In conclusion, when you visit Cabin John and Wheaton Regional Parks, or any park for that matter, don't litter and don't feed the wild animals. Perhaps if every park and zoo across the country had a Porky or a Billy for guidance, we would have fewer safety concerns and less trouble keeping these places clean.

Chapter 23

# A-MoCo-an Horror Story

## *Behind the Scenes of* The Blair Witch Project *with Eduardo Sánchez and Matt Blazi*

Horror movie fans, have I got a chapter for you. Not only am I going to talk about the story behind *The Blair Witch Project*, but I'm also here to talk about the Blair Witch Experience. This spooky, informative tour takes you through the filming locations for the movie and might even feature surprise visits from cast and crew members. Where does this tour take place? Right here in the teeth-chattering, spine-tingling, suburban depths of Montgomery County. And at the center of it all are a director and one of his most devoted fans.

Let's rewind this tale fifty-some years back to 1972. After moving from Cuba to Spain, four-year-old Eduardo Sánchez and his family moved a second time to the Long Branch Apartments in Takoma Park. He started to acclimate and learn English at Rolling Terrace Elementary School, a process he found easier with the help of English-language TV shows like *Buck Rogers in the 25th Century*, *What's Happening!!* and *Three's Company*. "I learned slang and how people talked here by watching all those shows," Sánchez said. "*Emergency!* was my favorite. It was so cool, it made me want to be a fireman."

Though his family didn't have a lot of money, Sánchez had two hardworking and supportive parents and a happy, adventurous childhood. He and his friends would hang out at the Wheaton Plaza and, later, the Westfield Wheaton Mall, playing games at the Time-Out arcade and eating ice cream at Farrell's. They also spent time playing in the creek behind his apartment complex—to his mother's chagrin, since he would usually come back wearing wet, muddy, smelly clothes. Little Sánchez loved a good mystery, such as why there was a room in their basement full of cinder blocks or why their local park looked like a crime scene on one of his visits. "My friend and I found bloody tissues and a couple of sticks with nails in them," Sánchez said. "We loved to play detectives, so we made up a story of what must have happened."

Sánchez realized his passion for the big screen at eight years old when he went to the theater to see a new release called *Star Wars*. He became totally consumed. He sought out and read whatever print materials he could find on how the film was made and what special effects were used. He also subscribed to *Starlog* magazine and began following the careers of directors Steven Spielberg and George Lucas.

As a little kid, Sánchez dreaded watching horror movies. He recalled being traumatized by the first one he ever saw, in which a black-and-white monster chased and caught a girl before eating her. He still remembers how scared he was watching the girl's leg dangle out of the monster's mouth, then disappear. In another instance, his mother decided to teach him a cautionary lesson about the dangers of the Devil by getting the family together to watch *The Exorcist*. "It was like watching a documentary from my mom's lap. That movie stuck with me, and I never watched it again until I was an adult," Sánchez said. "It's masterfully made, but I still don't like watching it."

Sánchez has had a love-hate relationship with the horror genre. As a kid, if he believed what creepy imagery he was watching was real, then it was a lot scarier. Still, he loved watching *In Search of…*, a show that catered to his love of the paranormal, supernatural and anything related to Bigfoot.

As a student at Wheaton High School in the 1980s, Sánchez got the chance to work at one of the first TV studios at any school in the county. He worked on lighting, editing, writing and directing under his teacher, Mr. Baron. Sánchez said, "Mr. Baron worked behind the scenes at a real TV station before coming to the school. He made me believe my passion was a real career—so now I was going to be a filmmaker."

Sánchez graduated from Wheaton as the class of 1987's "Most Likely to Succeed." Then he was off to Montgomery College and, later, studied film at the University of Central Florida, where he met and became friends with fellow student Daniel Myrick. The two didn't know it yet, but in 1991, a trip to see a movie from the *Nightmare on Elm Street* franchise would change their lives forever. As the friends walked out of the theater, they both had similar reactions. *Freddy's Dead* was fun and silly—but certainly not scary. When was the last time they had seen something really scary? Both men found they had great impressions of *In Search of…* and a 1972 horror film called *The Legend of*

*Boggy Creek*. They headed to the video store, rented *The Legend of Boggy Creek* and several episodes of *In Search of…* and began a watching frenzy.

When they turned off the TV set, the two concurred. These docu-horrors had scared them in the 1970s, and they scared them in the 1990s, too. Then it hit them. Why couldn't they scare a modern audience just as these videos had scared them?

Thus, was conceived a simple yet groundbreaking idea for a movie. A group of friends go into the woods camping; they get lost; their bodies are never found. Years later, someone finds footage left behind from their cameras. "It made a lot of business sense, we could shoot it for a low budget and it was an original idea," Sánchez said.

What with other projects and schoolwork, it took a couple years for Sánchez and Myrick to get back into the idea, but in 1993, the two officially started working on what Sánchez calls the "best and cheapest idea for us." The pair began creating the legend of Elly Kedward, or the Blair Witch, a woman banished from her home in Blair, Maryland, to the forest for practicing witchcraft. According to the legend, the forest now serves as an epicenter of paranormal phenomena. It would also serve as the setting of three student filmmakers' doomed investigation.

Over four years of development, Sánchez and Myrick headed back up to Maryland to scout out possible filming locations. They eventually settled on Montgomery County's own Seneca Creek State Park to play the woods of Burkittsville, the most prominent location in the movie. "Seneca Creek made the most sense. It was decently isolated, but there were houses around us in case something went wrong," Sánchez said. "There was varied terrain, and it didn't look the same the whole way through, so we could make it look like a much bigger area than it really was."

By 1997, the team had cast three main actors—Heather Donahue, Michael Williams and Joshua Leonard—all playing fictionalized versions of themselves. Serendipitously, Sánchez's then girlfriend (and now wife), Stefanie, lived two miles from Seneca Creek State Park in Germantown, and she let her boyfriend and his team use her townhouse as a production office for free. The film was shot over eight days in October that year, leaving the production team with twenty-two hours of footage to consider.

After over a year of editing, the movie premiered at the Sundance Film Festival in January 1999. The showing impressed Artisan Entertainment, who agreed to distribute the film later that year. The team wanted the movie to be perfect, so they continued to add, cut and edit footage before *The Blair Witch Project*'s wide release date: July 30, 1999. Would six years of

Daniel Myrick (*left*) and Eduardo Sánchez (*right*) hang "stickmen" shortly before filming *The Blair Witch Project*. The stickman is used as the film's symbol. *Eduardo Sánchez and Matt Blazi.*

investments—the relatively little money they had scraped up and the hard work they had done—pay off in an eighty-one-minute film?

If you had talked to an eighteen-year-old Matt Blazi that summer, he would have said it did. He saw *The Blair Witch* for the first time at a theater in rural central Pennsylvania. Blazi had this to say about his experience:

> *There are certain days you remember in life. This was one of those theater experiences where I had to sit up front and close. The entire audience was glued to the screen. You could hear very little chatter or noise. Most of the people in the theater probably thought it was real. There were gasps, then the credits hit and then a good fifteen seconds of silence. All of a sudden, chatter started; the entire theater was chatting. Not much unsettles me because I'm an Eagle Scout, but I had to drive through the woods to get home, and I had to go to sleep with the light on. It was real; it was on a camcorder; it wasn't flashy. I could really relate to what it was like to be in the woods. It was a high. I wanted more, so I went back two days later. I got the stickman from the movie tattooed on my arm the first week of college.*

The actors portraying character Robin Weaver's search party pose for what will be a black-and-white photo for the movie, 1998. *Eduardo Sánchez and Matt Blazi.*

Blazi had seen and adored horror movies before, but the buildup to this one was something special. While looking through a message board online, he discovered a link to www.blairwitch.com, a mysterious site that told the story of three film students who disappeared while looking for the Blair Witch in 1994. The website had photos and footage from the trio and claimed that the documentation came from the Frederick County Police Department and anthropologists from the University of Maryland. Slowly, fan sites and message boards began picking up on the disappearances after finding the website, never getting a hint that Sánchez and Myrick had made the site to promote a made-up story.

Seeing that the directors' marketing methods were working, Artisan Entertainment stuck with the same strategy when it became involved in 1999. The first trailer for the film dropped with *Star Wars: Episode I—The Phantom Menace.* "They just turned the volume up and widened the scope," Blazi said. "[Artisan] leaned more into it being real, but they never came out and said, 'This was real.' It's a once-in-a-lifetime thing, lightning in a bottle."

Don't let his day job as a commercial loan portfolio manager fool you. When it comes to making horror movies, Blazi is one dedicated man.

Through attending various conventions, he became friends with his horror idol, George A. Romero, director of *Dawn of the Dead*. Romero cast him as a zombie extra in not one but two of the film's sequels. If you look at German and Japanese posters for *Survival of the Dead*, you'll see him as one of the zombies featured. Following Romero's death in 2017, Blazi has become involved with the George A. Romero Foundation, which provides scholarships for future independent filmmakers.

Through a mutual friend, Blazi became acquainted with Sánchez in 2012, and the two struck up a friendship over their shared love of the horror genre. In 2013, Blazi and another friend came up with an idea that would change the lives of many a *Blair Witch Project* fan: What if we went camping like they did in the movie while checking out all the filming locations?

The two agreed and invited Sánchez, who decided to come—but not before mentioning the unique trip during a guest appearance on a podcast. Hearing about the trip, a woman reached out to Blazi and asked if she and her son could join, too. The small group met up and toured around the filming locations, from Montgomery County to Frederick County to Baltimore County, before setting up camp in Patapsco State Park. Here, Blazi FaceTimed his friend and *Blair Witch Project* cast member Michael Williams, who cheerfully retold stories from behind the scenes to the campers.

Williams recalled eight days of guerrilla filmmaking through the Maryland woods back in 1997. At Seneca Creek State Park, Williams and his two costars experienced one of their worst nights on set. Since the actors were continually filming on their cameras to capture the found-footage shots, the crew had to use GPS and walkie-talkies to mark and direct the actors to where they wanted them to spend more time improvising an interaction. One day, while shooting at Seneca Creek, a rainstorm came and drenched the cast's sleeping area and gear. Blazi retold the story:

> *The walkie-talkies got so soaked that night that they couldn't reach the crew. Heather, Mike and Josh found a house and a couple who let them use their phone and fed them cookies and cocoa while they got a hold of the crew. Their biggest misstep was going in the rain; they could have had all their equipment washed out. The next day was windy and sunny. They only got one shot the day before.*

After Blazi came home from the fun and fascinating camping trip, he immediately went on Facebook and created a Facebook group for fans of the movie. Membership numbers creeped higher and higher as Sánchez

*Blair Witch Project* codirector Eduardo Sánchez makes a special guest appearance during the Blair Witch Experience. *Matt Blazi.*

invited cast and crew members to join and more fans discovered the page. When members asked if Blazi could lead another tour, and then another tour, and then several more tours after that, the Blair Witch Experience became an annual tradition. Seneca Creek State Park even got in on the fun by providing its own tour of Coffin Rock, a filming location off Black Rock Road near Darnestown. "We started at three, then got to six, then twelve, then twenty-four; attendance doubled every year," Blazi said. "Then we got a bus and started doing T-shirts. We average around thirty people now and got seventy-six people for the twentieth anniversary."

Blazi is the author of an intensely researched book called *8 Days in the Woods: The Making of the Blair Witch Project.* The book took him four years to complete, watching and rewatching over 140 hours of footage, copiously taking notes to make a timeline. He also tracked down and interviewed almost every cast and crew member involved with the film. What he found was that while some of the actors interviewed in the film were planted performers, others were just people walking on the street.

For example, in the film, Heather interviews a fisherman along the banks of Seneca Creek about one of the movie's subjects, Rustin Parr. This man is Ed Swanson, an actor friend of Sánchez who enjoys showing up with a fishing rod at Seneca Creek and surprising fans during the Blair Witch Experience. On the other hand, in 1997, an unsuspecting woman named Susie Gooch saw what she thought were three student filmmakers in a diner in Brunswick, Maryland, and decided to help them out with an interview when no one else seemed to be very receptive to their questions. With her three-year-old daughter, Ingrid, in tow, Susie answered Heather's questions about the Blair Witch, vaguely remembering real conversations she'd had about a witch and relaying the info to Heather. "Susie's friend called her one day in 1999 and said she was on *Good Morning America*. Her interview from almost two years ago was on TV!" Blazi recalled. "Susie and Ingrid are sweet people, Susie's like a second mom to me, and I went to Ingrid's wedding."

Both Sánchez and Blazi have had a wonderful time creating a community of cast members, crew members and the fans who come on Blazi's tour every October. Some of Blazi's favorite memories are his interactions with Eleanor Bateman, whose Colony Supply Center in Beallsville was a filming location back when it was called Staub's Country Inn. On multiple occasions, she has greeted his tour group with apple cider and cookies while they check out where the movie was filmed.

Since his many, many days and nights working on *The Blair Witch Project*, Sánchez has kept himself busy directing, writing and editing other projects. You might recognize his directing credits from TV shows like *Lucifer*, *American Horror Stories*, *Queen of the South* or my personal favorite, *Yellowjackets*. Some shows he has directed hide Easter eggs in his episodes based on mythological characters from *The Blair Witch Project*. "I remember my first episode of *Supernatural* had a beer called Elly's Beer and a bar called Rustin's. I think *FBI* also had a bar called Rustin's," Sánchez said.

Against the odds, a movie made for less than $1 million grossed almost $250 million worldwide. Sánchez says he feels blessed and grateful for all the love from fans and the underdog success he's had. He prides himself on the close bonds he has maintained with coworkers on other projects since then. Thanks to Blazi, he has been able to keep in touch with the cast, crew and fans as well as the legacy of the film. About Blazi, Sánchez had this to say:

> He's a go-getter and loves the movie. He did a great job on his book, and I'm so grateful to him for his intense interest and hard work. He's the one who reconnects everyone in the cast and crew: he's the hub. Matt is always respectful, not pushy. Some fans want too much. They cross the line and become obnoxious, they don't respect my privacy—but Matt does. His heart is in the right place, and I'm honored that my movie is so important to him. He's helped me to gain perspective over the years on the movie and the fanbase. He's a good shepherd of the Blair Witch legacy.

Want to learn more about *The Blair Witch Project* and the Blair Witch Experience? Check out Matt Blazi's book, *8 Days in the Woods: The Making of The Blair Witch Project*; join the Blair Witch Experience group on Facebook; or sign up for the tour at www.blairwitchexperience.com. If you haven't already, make sure to watch the movie, too! In honor of the movie's twenty-fifth anniversary, Blazi has been planning for a tour like none before it, while as of this writing, Sánchez has been working on a special Blu-ray edition of *The Blair Witch Project*. I'm afraid if I reveal much more, I'll end up like Heather, Josh and Mike, lost forever in the vast and cursed wilderness of MoCo…

PART V

# THE COUNTRY AND THE ROADS

## Chapter 24

# THE FAMILY TREE OF BUTLER'S ORCHARD

On the outskirts of Germantown, locals in the Washington, D.C. area allow themselves out of their business formal attire and out of their high-rise apartments to catch a glimpse of how a bucolic lifestyle looks. We can come here to Butler's Orchard to pick our own apples, take a hayride or find our favorite bacon jam at the farm market. Without three generations of the Butler family, none of these little wonders would be possible.

Long before these three generations of the Butler family started growing trees, their ancestors worked in an industry where chopping them down was necessary. According to the 1850 U.S. census, Caleb Butler was a carpenter who worked in construction in Fleming County, Kentucky, before moving with his family to farm in Terre Haute, Indiana. His son, George Butler, would own a sawmill nearby, and George's son Roy Butler started out as a sawmiller as well. In the early 1900s, Roy left Indiana with his wife and three young children for North Dakota, where he went on to sell both lumber and real estate.

Roy's son George, named after his grandfather, would be the one to finally move away from the lumber industry. This George would spend time as a mechanic in North Dakota before moving to Maryland and becoming not a sawyer but a lawyer. Now, I could do a whole chapter on genealogy if I wanted, but I'll spare you by stopping at lawyer George's son, George Jr. This is where the Butler's Orchard story truly begins.

George Butler Jr. was born in 1928 in Washington, D.C., and grew up not on a rural farm near Germantown but in the affluent Silver Spring neighborhood of Seven Oaks. In high school, George impressed his classmates as an active member of the Montgomery Blair High School community, graduating in 1946 as vice president and director of student activities. One of his classmates was Shirley Brown, a childhood friend who lived a few neighborhoods over in Woodside. The two graduated and kept in touch as he went on to the University of Maryland (UMD) to study horticulture and she studied architecture and mathematics at Penn State University. Both George and Shirley graduated in 1950, and that same year, the two came back to Montgomery County and were married.

While 1950 brought some wonderful milestones for the couple, they also faced a whirlwind of challenges. George bought a thirty-seven-acre farm near Germantown on June 21, 1950, at the age of twenty-one, only eleven days after his commencement ceremony at UMD. Four days after he bought the property, the Korean War began, and George decided to enlist. He was stationed in Germany for two years but would return home for the annual peach harvest.

In the early days of Butler's Orchard, George worked for the post office to make extra income. The farm, then twenty-five acres, started out with a field of peaches and a mid-eighteenth-century log cabin where George and Shirley raised their four kids. Following advice from agents of the University of Maryland Extension, they started growing and selling fruits and vegetables. Shirley would sell some of their fruits at a roadside stand next to the house, while more of their products would go to be sold at the local Cider Barrel. The family upgraded their stand to a chicken house and then a red barn in 1964. The following decade, they began to sell items besides fruits and vegetables at the farm market, such as cider and local honey. The structure was expanded in 1993 to the much larger building of today.

Hallie Butler-Van Horn's father, Wade Butler, grew up in the rustic-looking cabin that now sits next to the farm market. Hallie recalls that where the market now stands, her grandparents once had their first strawberry field. For years, Shirley sold their fruit from a stand—until the 1960s, when she and her husband figured out that people enjoyed the experience of coming out to the country to handpick their produce, an experience one couldn't find in a place like her hometown of Silver Spring. Thus the family came up with the revolutionary "pick-your-own" produce concept and began to draw more and more people to their farm.

Of George and Shirley's four children, three of them took up the business as adults, while their daughter, Carol, now resides in Kentucky. Meanwhile, Todd, Wade and Susan all got degrees in horticulture from the University

*Top*: Carol Butler poses with her mother, Shirley Butler, in front of the "Pick Your Own" sign, circa 1964. *Butler family*.

*Bottom*: A 1950s picture of the Butler family. *Left to right*: Todd, Shirley (holding Carol), George Jr. (holding Susan), Wade Butler. *Butler family*.

of Maryland. Todd primarily ran the farm market; Wade worked with his father closely in farming and production; and Susan, with her mind and savvy for business and money, worked in the business office. As the farm became more well-established, it didn't face much competition, as it was one of the only pick-your-own establishments close to Washington, D.C. Rather than competition, the Butlers found camaraderie by partnering with local and small businesses to sell their products at their farm market.

In 1980, the Montgomery County Agricultural Reserve was created to stop developers from encroaching on the rural areas of northern and western Montgomery County. Within the reserve, the government allowed only one house per twenty-five acres. Not only did this discourage developers and protect much of Montgomery County's natural landscape, but it also made the land around Butler's Orchard much cheaper to purchase. The family subsequently bought 250 acres of land, which helped Butler's Orchard become the prominent farm we know today. Now, after more than seventy years, the Butlers see customers who visited them in the 1950s bringing their great-grandchildren to visit their farm in the 2020s.

Shirley and George's grandchildren are the third generation of Butler family members to work at Butler's Orchard. Their daughter Carol Butler is president of the University of Cincinnati's Goering Center for Family and Private Business. According to Carol, only 10 to 15 percent of family-owned businesses make it successfully to the third generation. Hallie, who is the farm's purchasing and personnel manager, has seen farms fail because of inadequate mentorship and a lack of proper succession and transition planning. "My aunt points out from her experience that there are three main issues with generational transitions," Hallie explained to me. "There's lack of communication and trust, lack of preparation of the next generation and there's lack of mission and vision."

Perhaps it's not surprising, then, that Butler's has found success uncommon in the industry. Hallie looks up to her father, Wade, for how he has let her lead in the family business and acted as a constant adviser to her as she gained more autonomy. She initially worked in retail management, but fond childhood memories reminded her of life on the farm. "Riding dirt bikes with Dad, riding on Grandpa's tractor, running through irrigation sprinklers to cool down during the summer….Those were some of my favorite memories," Hallie said. "The way a strawberry field smells: there's nothing quite like it. Imagine the best strawberry candle or lotion and multiply it by a thousand. And the way the sun sets on a farm! I didn't realize how much I missed it until I moved away."

Butler's Orchard founder George Butler Jr. hold his son Todd while his father, George Sr., works on irrigation equipment, 1956. *Butler family.*

The Butlers' cabin, tractor and original thirty-seven acres of land in the 1950s. *Butler family.*

The twenty-first century has brought its own challenges for the Butler family and running Butler's Orchard. George passed away in 2000, leaving Shirley, Todd, Wade and Susan to run the business. Then, in 2010, tragedy struck when Todd passed away in a farming accident. Todd Butler's passing signaled a turning point for the Butler family. In the days following his sudden death, it took many people to adopt his responsibilities.

Seeing the event as a call to action, Hallie and her brothers Tyler and Ben put their energies into helping the family farm move forward. Hallie went back to school for a year to earn a certificate in business management and then jumped back in with her brothers to start working full time at Butler's Orchard. "Tyler's general manager now, and Ben's been great with 'agritainment' as the farm and finance manager," Hallie said. "Ben is farmside, and Tyler and I are operations and customer-focused, but no one is ever alone in their role. If we need to jump in line to check people out or pop kettle corn, then we know how to jump in and help."

For the third generation of Butler's Orchard, digital technology like QuickBooks and Instagram has become vital to keeping the business running smoothly. Butler's Orchard launched its website and social media pages in 2012, expanding its reach beyond the word-of-mouth advertising

The Butler's Orchard Farm Market during the 1970s. *Butler family.*

they had relied on for more than sixty years. Hallie and her brothers worked on expanding their product line while cutting costs by making some of their own products. For example, Tyler introduced apple cider donuts, while Hallie introduced "Hallie's Heavenly" kettle corn into the farm market.

In the 2020s, the siblings have seen and taken on much change in the family. Shirley worked in the business office until her passing in 2020, and their aunt Susan passed away in 2022. In addition, the pandemic forced their business almost completely online. Shortly before Susan's passing, Hallie, Tyler and Ben bought Waters Orchard and Doc Waters Cidery from her and her husband, Wash, and took on experimenting with and learning how to make different ciders with their produce. Tart cherry cider, raspberry rosé and bourbon barrel cider make up just a few of their concoctions.

Hallie says that she admires the dedication, passion and work ethic she sees in the folks who come to work at Butler's. She appreciates that her parents let her leave the business to pursue different paths in healthcare and customer service before she made the decision to come back on her own.

So will there be a fourth generation at Butler's Orchard? As Hallie watches her mother, Angela, make caramel apples with Hallie's children, nieces and nephews, she wonders what paths her children might take and if it might lead them back to the log cabin in the woods. "The biggest thing our family strives for is legacy," Hallie said. "To keep this going for any of the future generations who want to take it on, to continue agriculture in Montgomery County."

# Chapter 25

# TURKEY THICKET

## *A Snapshot of Farm Life over One Hundred Years Ago*

With each passing year, it seems like Montgomery County gets more and more urban. Apartment buildings, shopping centers and Chick-Fil-A restaurants suddenly pop into view, and our area feels exponentially more metropolitan by the day. Outside of the bustling cities and caravans of Teslas, the Agricultural Historical Farm Park in Redland reminds us of a simpler time, when we had to make the fried chicken ourselves.

Along a rural stretch of Muncaster Road, the Farm Park takes visitors back to the early twentieth century, when Thaddeus Tyson Bussard owned the property. Thaddeus Bussard grew up near Ijamsville, Frederick County, Maryland, on a farm with five siblings. He would marry Ann Priscilla Murphy and raise five of his own children with her. Ann grew up as one of fourteen children, so perhaps having only five was a relief to her. Her parents, Horace and Charlotte Murphy, raised their pack of kids on a peach farm called Snow Hill. The Murphy family farm was located north of Clarksburg, along what is now Route 355. Some of the peaches grown there were shipped in feed bags to local stores for purchase, while the rest were taken a few miles north to Levi Price's distillery, where they were used to make peach brandy.

In Frederick County, Thaddeus tried to make a living as a merchant but was unsuccessful. He found that in Montgomery County, he could save money by buying more land for a cheaper price. So in 1888, Thaddeus and Ann bought a 260-acre farm for $7,000 and moved south to Redland with their four children, Louis, Felicia, Daisy and Harry. Ann would give birth to a fifth child, Bessie, inside the new farmhouse in 1891.

Ann Bussard (*front row, far right*) attends the Frederick Fair with seven of her siblings, circa 1930. Peering directly over her is Jefferson "Jeff" Murphy, the author's great-great-grandfather. *Ben and Diana Snouffer*.

The property already had a long history with the Magruder family. John Magruder—notably, the father of Colonel Zadok Magruder—began farming tobacco on the property in 1734. John's son Nathan Magruder would build a log house here in 1778; by the 1850s, Otho Magruder had replaced it with a stone house. By the time the Bussards acquired the property, the county's tobacco industry had collapsed and wheat had become the much more profitable crop. Montgomery County land records indicate that corn and rye were also produced on the property.

Otho Magruder receives credit for cofounding the Montgomery County Agricultural Society in 1846 and using guano to restore the farm's soil, damaged by years of tobacco planting. He also receives condemnation for owning twenty-seven slaves as listed in the 1850 Federal Slave Census. Black men, women and children were used to work the farm and harvest wheat for Magruder's profit during the mid-nineteenth century. According to the Maryland-National Capital Park and Planning Commission (M-NCPPC), which owns the Farm Park, the community of Newmantown sprang up next to the Magruder farm in 1879. Encouraged by Maryland's more welcoming attitude toward freed slaves, Albert and Mary Newman came from Virginia

The Bussard family at Turkey Thicket farm, circa 1898. *Carrie Boyd.*

to buy land for themselves here. Newmantown would become home to a thriving Black community and to the Newman family for almost one hundred years.

Now, back to the other side of the Farm Park. The Bussards referred to their farm as Turkey Thicket, as remembered by Bessie Bussard's great-granddaughter Carrie Boyd. Turkey Thicket changed drastically under the Bussards' ownership. In 1898, Thaddeus began remodeling the house, demolishing Otho Magruder's stone house and building a brand-new two-story frame house with bay windows on the original foundation. This Victorian house is the one that has been kept and restored by the M-NCPPC.

M-NCPPC historians elaborate that Thaddeus added a smokehouse, a granary, a double cornhouse, a blacksmith shop, a bank barn and many other features to the farm during his time there. The Bussards collected bacon from their pigs, ice from their pond when it froze and income from selling cream, butter and milk from their cows. This hard work would continue when Thaddeus passed down the property to his son Harry in 1924—only Harry would have more modern conveniences to work with, like electric appliances. As a child, Harry had to go outside to the privy to use the bathroom, but as an adult, he got the chance to use indoor plumbing inside the house when it was installed for the first time.

Harry and his wife, Katherine Lawson Bussard, had six daughters and three sons. Their oldest son, Harry Jr., was killed in a tragedy that happened inside the farmhouse. On Valentine's Day 1923, two-year-old Harry Jr. got hold of a set of matches while his mother was out of the room and accidentally lit himself on fire. He was taken to Montgomery General Hospital but died four days later.

Harry's children would help with manual tasks like feeding the chickens, collecting their eggs and milking the cows. In a 2008 interview for the Montgomery County Parks Department, Harry's daughter Edith Cross recalled to interviewer Alden Watts that she and her five sisters had to milk the cows before boarding the school bus every morning. "And if we didn't go to school, and we played sick, we was [*sic*] out in the field working," Cross said. The dinner bell was another fixture of Edith's life, used to summon her and her eight siblings to the house for meals or emergencies. She and her sister Mabel donated the dinner bell to the M-NCPPC after the organization bought the property in the late 1960s. Harry Bussard's family was the last to farm on the property before the M-NCPPC made the grounds part of the Agricultural Historical Farm Park.

Turkey Thicket still stands proudly on a hill overlooking Rock Creek and a vast greenery of trees and fields. More than two hundred years of raising children, animals and crops happened here, but the pastoral property now sits placidly. It's a wonderful place to come to reflect on your life and the lives of those who came before you.

# Chapter 26

# DAMASCUS'S DECLASSIFIED DINNER RECIPE GUIDE

How did we prepare our dinners in the times before Safeway, air fryers and Wawa Hoagiefest? In this chapter, you'll learn how Damascus locals made a meal before many of these luxuries existed. I found and adapted these recipes with thanks to *Our Bicentennial Cookbook*, published by the Bicentennial Commission of Damascus in 1976.

FAIRY BURDETTE WARFIELD submitted this potato puff recipe to the *Bicentennial Cookbook* in 1976. The author was her mother, Beda King Burdette, who lived in the Woodfield neighborhood just south of Damascus and wrote the recipe in 1912. In 2023, the King-Burdette family celebrated their eighty-eighth annual family reunion!

### Potato Puffs
*(adapted from Beda King Burdette, submitted by Fairy Burdette Warfield)*

*1 cup yeast*
*1 cup lard (or butter/Crisco) mixed w/1 cup hot mashed potatoes*
*1 scant cup sugar*
*2 eggs*
*1 cup milk*
*1 teaspoon salt*

Proof the yeast in a large bowl, then mix in the rest of the ingredients. Cover and let the mixture rise like a loaf of bread for forty-five minutes. Scoop mixture into a greased muffin pan and bake for thirty minutes at four hundred degrees Fahrenheit. On the likely chance you don't cook with lard on a regular basis, butter or Crisco works fine.

If preferred, grate parmesan cheese on top before baking like I did.

Floyd "Buddy" Burns and his wife, Ada, submitted their recipe to the cookbook in memory of Buddy's mother, Polly, otherwise known as Grace Sheckels Burns. According to a note accompanying the recipe, it was created in 1900.

### Baked Tomatoes
*(adapted from Grace "Polly" Burns, submitted by Ada and Buddy Burns)*

*2 pounds tomatoes*
*4 slices dry bread (toast)*
*3 tablespoons butter*
*1 grated onion*
*½ bell pepper, chopped*
*½ cup sugar*
*1 teaspoon salt, pepper to taste*

In a well-greased baking dish, place your tomatoes. Butter the toast, cut it into small squares, and then add them to the dish. Mix in onion, bell pepper and sugar. Season with salt and pepper, and then bake for twenty-five to thirty minutes at four hundred degrees Fahrenheit.

Feel free to use croutons if you want to skip a step, or you can make the toast yourself by baking the bread for three to five minutes at four hundred degrees in a toaster or air fryer. If you want to make the dish lighter, use less of the croutons or take them out altogether.

*Top*: Three longtime businesses located on Ridge Road in Damascus, circa 1950s. *Shirley Appleby.*

*Middle*: A sugar ration check issued by the Bank of Damascus. Supply shortages during World War II led to the U.S. government instituting food ration checks. *Shirley Appleby.*

*Bottom*: Built in 1909, this general store once served the rural community of Cedar Grove near Damascus. Cedar Grove Store is now a beer store and deli. *Shirley Appleby.*

Doris King submitted this recipe in memory of Mary Adella "Della" Moxley, who lived near Browningsville, west of Damascus. Della's husband, Emory, was a well-known repairman in the area. In the 1965 *Frederick News* article "Damascus Mower Expert Finds Business Changing," J. Pinoake Browning reported that Emory Moxley had been fixing lawn mowers in the area for over forty years despite losing his arm in a farming accident as a young man.

### Mince Meat
*(adapted from Della Burdette Moxley, submitted by Doris King Burdette)*

*3 pounds beef*
*¼ or ½ pound suet (or butter/shortening)*
*2 lemons (zest and juice)*
*2 pounds raisins*
*2 or 3 oranges and juice*
*1 can peaches (mashed)*

In one pan, cook the beef. In another pan, cook the rest of the ingredients together until the butter, suet or shortening is fully melted. Combine the beef and fruit mixture together. If the recipe is not sweet enough, the author recommends adding apples, currants or nutmeg if desired.

Meat and fruit make an odd pairing, but this dish ended up tasting fantastic. I substituted craisins for raisins and grapefruits for oranges. For seasoning, I used allspice, nutmeg, cinnamon, ginger and cloves.

You can also make the dish into a pie by wrapping and cooking the mincemeat in pastry dough. For my dish, I spooned the mixture into phyllo shells and cooked them in the oven for six minutes at 350 degrees. The mincemeat was hot and the shells were crispy, a delicious combo.

Lillian Burdette Miles lived in Damascus and was the wife of Roby Byrd Miles. The recipe she submitted is perhaps the oldest and one of the sweetest mentioned in the book. Miles wrote that these especially soft cookies date to about 1800.

### Old-Fashioned Brown Sugar Cookies
*(adapted from a recipe submitted by Lillie Miles)*

¾ cup melted lard (otherwise, butter or shortening)
1 pound brown sugar
2 eggs
Approx. 5½ cups flour
½ pint sour cream
½ teaspoon baking soda (stirred in sour cream)
1 teaspoon vanilla extract
Pinch of salt

Pour the butter or shortening you have over the brown sugar. Add both eggs, flour, sour cream and baking soda, vanilla extract and a pinch of salt. The cookies will be best if you roll them thick and use a cookie cutter to cut them. Bake for ten minutes at about 350 degrees, then decorate with raisins and granulated sugar.

I'm not a raisin guy, so instead I mixed in chocolate chips and oats prior to baking and used the base to make oatmeal chocolate chip cookies. Results? Sensational.

The *Bicentennial Cookbook* not only offers tons of recipes but also a glimpse at the foods many Montgomery Countians enjoyed one hundred years ago. In a time when we relied much more on hunting for our food, blackbirds and squirrels were among the ingredients mentioned in some recipes. In 1915, a typical Thanksgiving dinner consisted of boiled cod, roast turkey with chestnut stuffing, plum pudding, potato balls and ice cream. For Christmas, typical items were oysters on the half shell, cream of celery soup, roast turkey, stewed onions and pumpkin pie.

These feasts would go against the diet recommended by Dr. T.J. Ritter in his 1913 guide *The People's Home Medical Book*. To start the day, Ritter would suggest three ounces of lean meat, one ounce of unbuttered bread and a cup of tea or coffee. For "early luncheon" he recommends a soft-boiled egg with an ounce of bread, and for "afternoon luncheon" he advises a thick water cracker with milk or tea. For dinner, you could have a cup of clear soup, some fish and lean meat and small quantities of vegetables. Then, for the grand finale of dessert… a single fruit.

# Chapter 27

# It's Not Just the Street You Live On

On July 23, 2021, the descendants of Geneva Mason and William Dove looked up proudly as workers replaced streets signs bearing the names of Confederate military officers with "Geneva Mason Road," "Geneva Mason Court" and "William Dove Court." Dove and Mason were gaining this recognition in honor of their work in building and preserving the historically Black community of Scotland, located off Seven Locks Road in Potomac. These new street names represent a visual update of Montgomery County's values and history and the people who made the county what it is today.

Yes, sometimes naming methods aren't that deep. They can be quite obvious. Laytonsville Road leads to Laytonsville, and University Boulevard leads to the University of Maryland. When you drive down Dickerson Church Road, you're in Dickerson—and oh, look, there's a church. These road names don't give you much of a puzzle to solve.

On the other hand, if you're driving along Route 28 by the Kentlands, you might wonder why there's a road leading into the neighborhood that begins with four consonants. This road, Tschiffely Square Road, requires a little more research. Before the Kentlands was acquired by its namesake, the eccentric and well-off Otis Kent, the Swiss American family of Frederick Tschiffely Sr. (pronounced shih-*fay*-lee) owned and farmed the land here.

The Tschiffelys were a prominent family in Montgomery County during the nineteenth century. Frederick Sr.'s son, Frederick Jr. opened the Tschiffely Pharmacy in Washington, D.C., in 1874, and it remains one of the oldest

Darnestown Road before it was paved and became known as Route 28. This picture, circa 1910, shows the road as it winds through Darnestown. *Photo by Lewis Reed, courtesy of Jeanne Gartner.*

operating drugstores there after 150 years. Another son, Elgar, gained notoriety as the last surviving Confederate soldier in Montgomery County, while a third son, Wilson, owned and operated the Seneca Stone Mill. The graffiti-covered ruins of Wilson Tschiffely's mill are located at the end of Tschiffely Mill Road by the Potomac River.

Driving up to Montgomery Village, you'll pass the oddly named Lost Knife Road. Did someone drop their plastic utensil coming out of the Wendy's down the street? Negatory: Lost Knife comes from one of the oldest documented land tracts in the area, known as the Lost Knife. While the reasoning behind the name is unclear, Maryland land records tell us that the 150-acre property was surveyed on May 30, 1741, for a man named John Rawlins. You're more likely to recognize the names of famous racehorses—Gate Dancer, Carry Back, Foolish Pleasure—assigned to the streets of Germantown's Hoyles Mill Village or North Potomac's Fox Hills Green neighborhood.

Like the roads mentioned at the beginning of this chapter, Good Hope, Emory Grove and Brickyard Roads commemorate three of the dozens of historically Black communities that have existed in Montgomery County. You might not look twice at such serene-sounding names, and that's great news for the people who live on those streets. Residents who live on Olney's Morningwood Drive and Glenmont's Terrapin Drive aren't so lucky, according to a 2019 news report by WJLA's Kevin Lewis.

These signs have continued to be targeted for theft; some signs are stolen once every month. The situation had gotten so bad with Germantown's Blunt Road and Colesville's Stoner Drive signs that Montgomery County's Traffic Engineering and Operations Division was forced to remove the vowels from the signage so that passersby wouldn't be tempted by any marijuana-related terminology. "Blnt Road" and "Stnr Drive" just don't capture the same attention.

More prominent roads like Father Hurley Boulevard, Grosvenor Lane and Gude Drive were named for notable figures from twentieth-century Montgomery County history. Father Leonard Hurley got to see his name on the sign for I-270's Exit 16 for twenty-eight years before his death in 2015. He was a founding pastor of Mother Seton Catholic Church on the boulevard that now bears his name, serving there from 1974 to 1987. Years before coming to Germantown, he had acquired international recognition for narrating the Requiem Mass of President John F. Kennedy on a worldwide radio and TV broadcast.

Then there's Gilbert H. Grosvenor (pronounced *groh*-vuh-nurr), the father of Grosvenor Lane. Grosvenor was the first full-time editor at *National Geographic* magazine, where he worked for fifty-five years, and he became president of the National Geographic Society in 1920. While Grosvenor holds his own claim to fame due to his heavy role in building and growing the National Geographic Society, he doesn't get as much attention as his wife Elsie's father. His father-in-law was the famous Alexander Graham Bell, who invented the telephone in 1876.

East and West Gude Drives have always perplexed drivers with their pronunciation. Is it Gude like "rude" or Gude like "Rudy"? Well, Gilbert

In North Bethesda, I-70S approaches what was then I-270 (now the I-270 Spur) in 1969. I-70S would be renamed I-270 in 1975. *U.S. House Committee on Transportation & Infrastructure.*

Gilbert H. Grosvenor, highly influential president of the National Geographic Society from 1920 to 1954. His father-in-law was the famous inventor Alexander Graham Bell. *LOC.*

Gude (pronounced like Rudy) grew up on his father Adolph Gude's farm and nursery on a stretch of what is now East Gude Drive. Gilbert Gude grew up to become a successful politician, eventually getting elected to the U.S. House of Representatives from Maryland's Eighth Congressional District. In other words, he has the same job title Representative Jamie Raskin does as of this writing. Gilbert Grosvenor, Gilbert Gude—is there a *Gilbert Grape* reference in here, too?

Any *Star Trek* fans reading this book? The Redland Park neighborhood near Derwood was themed after the series. Three of its streets were named after *Antares*, *Reliant* and *Intrepid*, starships featured throughout the *Star Trek* franchise. Tribble Way and Stratos Lane also pay homage to the series, and Fontana Lane honors D.C. Fontana, a screenwriter for five decades on various *Star Trek* series.

How about Beatlemaniacs? If that's you, then you might consider moving to Olney's Manor Oaks neighborhood, where all the streets are named in honor of the Beatles: Abbey Manor Drive after the band's *Abbey Road* album; Sutcliff Terrace after the band's original bass guitarist, Stuart Sutcliffe; and Starkey Drive after Richard Starkey, the birth name of drummer Ringo Starr. Dive deeper into the Beatles' history and you'll discover that the Quarrymen, John Lennon's musical predecessor to the Beatles, gave their name to Quarrymen Terrace.

Whether you live in a cul-de-sac named after a trend from the 1960s or you're constantly receiving crime alerts about street sign bandits, the name of your road has a story. It's not just the street you live on; it's also the sense of history and personality infused by developers into your neighborhood.

## Chapter 28

# THAT JOHN DENVER SONG
# "TAKE ME HOME, CLOPPER ROAD"

Clopper Road inspired a certain "mountain mama" song, but you won't be driving over any mountains here. The road meanders lightly through Gaithersburg, Germantown and Boyds, a pleasant drive that won't make your ears pop. It was this pleasant drive along Clopper Road that gave one man the idea to write one of the biggest country songs of all time.

In 1970, Bill Danoff and his girlfriend Taffy Nivert were a musical duo called Fat City and looking to expand their careers. On the way to Nivert's family reunion in Gaithersburg, she drove them up Clopper Road. Clopper Road was much more of a country road at the time and reminded Danoff of his upbringing along the rustic routes of western Massachusetts. He began working on a new song with help from Nivert, eventually settling on West Virginia as the setting for "Take Me Home, Country Roads."

In December that year, they showed off the new song to country singer John Denver, who was performing for multiple days at the Cellar Door Nightclub in Georgetown. According to a 2020 article by NBC4 Washington's Mark Segraves, the couple had already written a song Denver had recorded called "I Guess He'd Rather Be in Colorado." Denver apparently loved "Take Me Home, Country Roads," and after working with the couple to adjust some of the lyrics, he brought Danoff and Nivert onstage to perform the song for the first time in public on December 30, 1970.

After its commercial release in 1971, "Country Roads" arguably became Denver's signature song, peaking at no. 2 on the Billboard Hot 100 and

Clopper Road, circa 1960s. Native Americans once used this road as a trail. In 1951, the bridge pictured here was built over Great Seneca Creek. *MCHS.*

John Denver meets with President Gerald R. Ford in the Oval Office of the White House in 1975. *National Archives, Gerald R. Ford White House Photographs.*

becoming the state song for West Virginia in 2014. Danoff and Nivert would go on to a bigger band with greater success as singers in Starlight Vocal Band. They are remembered as a one-hit wonder for their immensely popular 1976 song "Afternoon Delight," which you may recognize from the 2004 hit comedy *Anchorman: The Legend of Ron Burgundy*. During the 1970s, Danoff continued to write songs for other artists like Emmylou Harris. Together, they wrote Harris's song "Boulder to Birmingham," released in 1975.

It turns out Nivert has more than one unique connection to a road in Montgomery County. She's a descendant of the King family, and her family is the namesake of Kings Valley and Kingstead Roads near Damascus. It seems only fitting that in a county getting more and more suburban by the day, these roads are still country ones.

Consider this, too, music fans. If you're not into John Denver but you are into Darius Rucker, go check out the Poolesville Golf Course. His band Hootie and the Blowfish filmed part of the music video for "Only Wanna Be with You" here. On the other side of the county, Silver Spring serves as the namesake for Fleetwood Mac's song "Silver Springs." Band member Stevie Nicks saw a sign on the freeway for Silver Spring and was so enamored of the enchanting name that it inspired her to write a new song.

PART VI

# LESSONS LEARNED

## Chapter 29

# THE POWER OF GOLD FEVER

For this chapter, let's start by considering the family of Mary Ann Cecil in the 1850 United States Federal Census.

According to the 1850 census, Mary Cecil lived in the Clarksburg district with her parents, Richard and Catherine Thompson; six of her siblings; and three of her children. Her other two kids were staying with their grandparents Samuel and Ann Cecil when this census was taken. But where was Mary's husband?

Luckily, it's not hard to miss a guy whose name is Hammedatha, a Persian name for the lesser-known father of Haman. If you've been to Hebrew school or Sunday school, you might recognize Haman as the man who tried to wipe out all the Jews in Persia but was thwarted by Queen Esther.

It's hard to think highly of a man named after the father of an attempted murderer, and even harder when you find out that Hammedatha Cecil apparently abandoned his wife and five kids for gold in California. He may have originally promised to return to his family or send for them once he established himself, but he never did. He ended up marrying another woman he met out in California and spending the rest of his life there with her. Mary also remarried, but for many years, her children lived with Hammedatha's parents, possibly because she could not afford to care for all of them, as was more common in the nineteenth century.

Hammedatha's fever for gold in California fractured his family in Maryland. While he craved gold in the West, other Marylanders didn't need to rush far for the precious ore. In 1849, news began to spread that gold had

Gold wasn't the only mineral found at the Maryland Gold Mine. Galena and quartz were found at the site of the mine in 1937. *MCHS.*

been found on a farm in Olney, and the fever spread across the county. Two years after the Civil War, the Maryland Mining Company dug out the shafts of the Maryland Gold Mine near Great Falls.

In his book *Montgomery County Gold Fever*, author Walter A. Goetz points out eleven gold mine locations within a few miles of Great Falls. On Sunday, April 15, 1866, Washington's *Sunday Herald* reported on the coinage metals found in the Great Falls area:

> *Several leads have been discovered, and some show gold to the naked eye in sufficient quantities to warrant their working by machinery. There is in this city a number of specimens brought from there, which bid fair to be the forerunner of rich leads of gold, silver and copper ores.*

While the gold mines offered locals an exciting method to make money, they could be perilous under the right circumstances. On the night of June 15, 1906, George Elliott and Charles Eglin were preparing dynamite in a shack at the Maryland Gold Mine when a torch fell over and ignited, lighting a wick.

Immediately realizing their mistake, the two of them rushed to exit the shack. Elliott made it out, but Eglin was too late, and the explosion killed him. The *Montgomery County Sentinel* reported the following week that people

The Maryland Gold Mine at Great Falls after the explosion of June 15, 1906. *MCHS.*

from nine miles away in Rockville could sense the blast. Upon feeling the explosion, one person assumed that a family member had fallen out of bed, while another local theorized that the booming had come from their chimney collapsing. One local even postulated that the shaking was from an aftershock that traveled across the country from San Francisco.

Gold continued to be mined at the Maryland Gold Mine until 1940, when the amounts found there were too low for the business to make a profit. According to Goetz, the Maryland Gold Mine was the last such site to close in Montgomery County. During the late nineteenth and early twentieth centuries, gold mines were actively operating farther out in places like Boyds, Bethesda and Rockville.

You can still spot the ruins of the Maryland Gold Mine down a short trail at the corner of MacArthur Boulevard and Falls Road. Is it really that surprising that Potomac—one of the most affluent places in the country— has several gold mines hiding out among its many mansions? In a place where opulence is prevalent, the mines lie untouched and unproductive, symbols of a golden past outshined by the gilded present.

Chapter 30

# Garrett Park and the Troublesome Toilet

The town of Garrett Park, Maryland, was named after Robert Garrett, president of the B&O Railroad when the town was founded. Maryland's youngest county, Garrett County, bears the name of Robert's father, John Work Garrett, who preceded his son as president of the B&O. John Garrett had served for fourteen years as president when he was honored with the namesake in 1872.

By the end of the nineteenth century, Garrett Park had become a small haven for people working in Washington, D.C. The tiny town was the brainchild of the Metropolitan Investment & Building Company. In 1887, the company seized the opportunity to build a suburban community along the Metropolitan Branch of the B&O Railroad. Residents of Garrett Park could deal with fewer crowds than in the city, enjoy a mere thirty-minute commute into Washington and avoid the packed, disease-ridden urban environment.

Between 1890 and 1894, Garrett Park grew to include a post office, a wooden schoolhouse and a railroad station. Many of the town's original Victorian homes still stand. Before her passing in 1961, resident Hattie Defandorf recalled in her memoirs that the town during the 1890s was a "children's paradise," a great place for youngsters to play in the woods and farmland around the community without the worry of getting hit by an automobile.

If Garrett Park was a safety bubble, then the arrival of the Sprigg family was the needle threatening to pop it. In 1898, panic broke out after more than fourteen thousand people in Philadelphia were exposed to typhoid fever when sewage leaked into the city's drinking water. Around the same

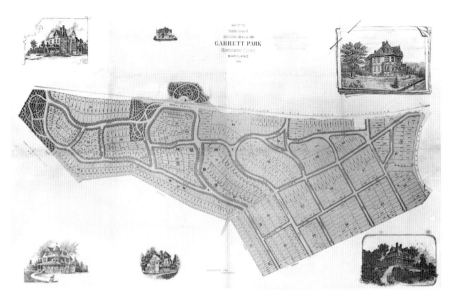

Drawing based on Garrett Park in 1891, submitted for the Charles E. Peterson Prize in 2000. *LOC.*

time, well-to-do New Yorkers James and Grace Sprigg moved into a house on Garrett Park's Waverly Avenue. James was the grandson of a U.S. congressman, while Grace was the daughter of a millionaire corn starch manufacturer.

While their neighbors relied on outdoor privies, Grace chose to set up a water closet connected to a septic tank. At the time, Americans more commonly used outhouses because they could be placed far from houses and water sources. The concept of indoor plumbing was new to the people of Garrett Park, and it made them fearful that the Spriggs's excrement would leach into the groundwater and poison the wells used for drinking water. The residents of Garrett Park did not want their neighborhood to become the next Philadelphia.

Typhoid fever was nothing to take lightly back before modern sanitation practices and antibiotics. An 1889 report by the Montgomery County Medical Society stated that in the past twelve months, mortality rates for the bacterial diseases dysentery and diphtheria amounted to about 3 percent each. The mortality rate for Montgomery Countians who contracted typhoid had skyrocketed to 20 percent.

So what did the people of Garrett Park do to prevent typhoid fever? They incorporated their town on May 4, 1898. Led by its new official government, the town passed one of its first ordinances: to regulate outhouses and ban

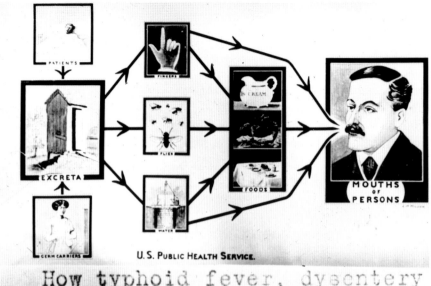

A diagram of how typhoid fever spreads from person to person, circa 1920s. *U.S. Public Health Service via Library of Congress.*

4710 Waverly Avenue, Garrett Park. This house was once the home of the Sprigg family, whose plumbing played a major part in the town's founding. *M-NCPPC.*

the use of "privy sinks, cesspools and other depositories of filth," as the *Montgomery County Sentinel* reported in one article from June 30, 1899.

Grace Sprigg refused to stop using her indoor plumbing, so a health officer came and disconnected the pipe to her septic tank. After a year of fighting the case against her controversial commode, Sprigg lost on June 20, 1899, when the Maryland Court of Appeals sided with the town of Garrett Park, citing the need to protect the neighborhood from disease. Defeated by their own community, the Spriggses moved back to New York in 1900, just two years after they arrived. Their time as locals was short, but certainly helped to make Garrett Park the town it is today.

# Chapter 31

# THE GAITHERSBURG LATITUDE OBSERVATORY

A s mechanical engineer William Sanford Nye once claimed in the intro to the ever popular TV show *Bill Nye the Science Guy*, "Science rules!" If those two words didn't convince you back when you were in seventh grade science class, perhaps this chapter will instead.

Let's talk about the Gaithersburg Latitude Observatory. It doesn't seem like much at first. It's located in a tiny park off DeSellum Avenue, and it's only thirteen square feet in area. Don't let its size fool you: this humble structure has a monumental place in international earth science history.

From 1899 to 1982, this National Historic Landmark was one of only six observatories in the world designed by the International Polar Motion Service to study the earth's wobble. Gaithersburg held this unique distinction along with Cincinnati, Ohio; Mizusawa, Japan; Charjui, Russian Turkestan; Ukiah, California; and Carloforte, Italy. In the decade prior to the observatory's creation, scientists discovered that the earth wobbles on its polar axis like an unsteady top, causing variations in latitude known as Chandler's wobble. All six observatories sat on the same line of latitude so that researchers could make uniform, accurate calculations over time.

Edwin Smith, a resident of nearby Rockville, was primarily responsible for the construction of the observatory and for recording measurements there. Smith was also chief of the Instrument Division of the U.S. Coast and Geodetic Survey, which is now known as the National Oceanic and Atmospheric Administration (NOAA). When he slid open the roof of the observatory, he could use his telescope to measure the location of a

International Latitude Observatory in Gaithersburg, circa 1900. *City of Gaithersburg.*

constant set of stars, as his fellow researchers from the other observatories did the same.

In 1915, after sixteen years, the observatory closed due to federal budget constraints, but seventeen years later, the U.S. government decided to reopen the site. The task of running the entire operation was given to twenty-nine-year-old Earl Larkin Williams, a brilliant academic with a passion for astronomical research and an enviable résumé of experiences, like traveling to observe a solar eclipse in Durango, Mexico, at the age of twenty.

From the time the U.S. government hired Williams to run the observatory in Gaithersburg, his life revolved around taking careful notes of the locations of the stars above DeSellum Avenue. Before Williams began working there, he had instructed students in mathematics and astronomy at institutions like Ohio State University and Muhlenberg College. At the observatory, he began working away, squinting through a telescope to measure the distance between pairs of stars for six hours every night he could. If the night sky became too cloudy, Williams was out of luck.

In 1932, Williams and his new wife, Helen, moved into a house provided by the government next door to the observatory. This house later expanded as their family grew to include four children, who got into reading books

*Left*: Tripod at the International Latitude Observatory. *City of Gaithersburg.*

*Below*: Home built for the head researcher at the International Latitude Observatory, circa 1900. *City of Gaithersburg.*

rather than tracking the stars like their father. Williams encouraged the public to ask him questions about his work at the observatory but would not let anyone enter. If one person accidentally bumped into the telescope while visiting, they could mess up the focal configuration of the instrument and ruin the effort Williams had made.

Aside from its scientific significance, the observatory also holds a place in history as a symbol of unity across the world. Not even World War II could stop the observatories in the Axis nations of Germany and Japan from communicating with the Allies' station in Gaithersburg.

Astronomers would continue looking up through the telescope here until the government permanently shut down the observatory in 1982. Computerization had led to great advances in astronomical research practices, rendering the telescope in Gaithersburg obsolete for these purposes. Although the government no longer uses the observatory, curious minds can visit the tiny building to get a better understanding of how Edwin Smith and Earl Williams performed their duties. Within the same park, visitors can check out the Observatory RM-1 Monument as well, which has been used by the NOAA since 1966 to evaluate its global positioning systems, or GPSs.

Chapter 32

# Fifteen Years and Thirty-Two Tall-Grassed Acres of Fourth School

At the woodsy intersection of South Glen and Norton Roads in Potomac, there are three long driveways. One leads to a house, another to a synagogue and the last one stretches on and down to an eerie complex of buildings. Some of these buildings look like repurposed mobile homes, while one of the bigger ones looks like a giant snowflake made of hexagons. There's a library, about a dozen classrooms and a gymnasium, even a pool house, but not a student or teacher to be seen around any of them—all the makings for a fun, fine education, now lost to time.

Hidden in plain sight, Fourth Presbyterian School sat on thirty-two acres of forest, fields and hills, seemingly cut off from the outside world. Khaki pants or plaid skirts didn't stop us kids from running headlong into the muddy creek that ran through the campus to play freeze tag or say hi to the tadpoles. They didn't stop us until a loud shout from one of the teachers had us scrambling and tripping up the side of the ravine to get back into our metaphorical "goody two-shoes" so we wouldn't get a yellow card back in class.

Fourth School, as many of us called it, was founded in 1999 by the Fourth Presbyterian Church in Bethesda to "extend its covenant of Christian education" and prepare its students for college from an early age. When it first opened, the school only offered prekindergarten through first grade. By 2012, the school had a full preschool, elementary school and middle school, with plans for a four-hundred-student-capacity building that would accommodate not only quadruple the number of students but a high school as well.

Taking advantage of its rural setting, Fourth School had many traditions, like Nature Club, which offered students a chance to explore the beautiful woods, streams and wildlife around them. During the school's earlier years, staff, students and their families enjoyed annual campouts complete with a village of tents, s'mores and tournaments of gravel (kind of an eyes-closed mix of "the floor is lava" and tag). In the 2010s, science teacher TJ Fleming set up a garden to teach students how to properly care for plants and grow them over the course of a semester. One fifth grade class set up bluebird boxes around the campus and monitored them for activity. Some got bluebirds. Others got ants.

Despite its relatively low number of students, Fourth's landscape was vast. One day, after a game of manhunt in PE class, in which students played hide-and-go-seek using the entire campus, one girl failed to show up to her next class for half an hour—before suddenly appearing to her bewildered classmates as if nothing had happened. As it turned out, she had gone almost all the way to the edge of campus and only continued to hide because she was too far away to hear the coach's whistle echoing through the valley.

The Myers siblings' first day at Fourth Presbyterian School, September 2007. *Author's collection.*

Back in 1911, the area surrounding Rockville (now Richard Montgomery) High School (*center*) looked much like the wooded area surrounding Fourth Presbyterian School in 2011. *Photo by Lewis Reed, courtesy of Jeanne Gartner.*

Other fond memories of the campus include Summer Splash, a summer day camp for Fourth students with water games and cake-eating contests; the Fun Run, an annual run for both students and staff to raise money for a nonprofit called Romanian Christian Enterprises; and, more notably, Friday Finales, schoolwide celebrations held on the last Friday of each month with a different theme every time. There was Hoedown Day, on which everyone would dress up like Old West characters and square dance in the gymnasium. Then there was Tacky Day, when the sixth graders came to school dressed like the first graders had picked out their clothes.

At the end of the 2013–14 school year, with about one hundred students across preschool, elementary and middle school, the Fourth Presbyterian School ceased its educational operations. In its fifteen years, the school had hosted guest speakers like NBA champion shooting guard Adrian Branch as well as surfer and author Bethany Hamilton. In 2011, Fourth School sent seventh grader Susanna Yau to the Scripps National Spelling Bee, and in 2013, it celebrated second-grade teacher Jeanne Minnick as she won Gilder Lehrman History Teacher of the Year for Maryland. The school offered a stellar education, inside and outside its four walls.

As of this writing, the thirty-two acres of this former grade school is slated to be developed into a senior living community called Heritage Potomac. I remember how strange the transition was at twelve years old when I traded in my Fourth School branded polos for Tame Impala and SpongeBob SquarePants T-shirts. It was even stranger realizing four hundred people were in my new seventh grade class versus the ten to twelve kids I'd expected every year. Will anything ever be stranger than watching it all disappear?

Chapter 33

# Montgomery County Personal Histories

## *Living over Eighty Years in MoCo*

More than one million people call Montgomery County, Maryland, home, but only a select number of them can say they've lived the long, amazing lives of the people in this chapter. I have had the great pleasure and honor of hearing four stories from four different county residents ranging in age from 85 to 105 years old. All of them have lived in the county for at least 85 years, seeing the area go through decades of change. One of them was alive during World War I!

Without further ado, here's our first story.

## Mr. Benjamin Snouffer

Benjamin George "Ben" Snouffer was born at home on October 10, 1938, in Potomac. The youngest of three children, he grew up along River Road, which was then a dirt road he walked along to catch the school bus at Piney Meetinghouse Road. From there in Potomac to St. Martin's School in Gaithersburg, the trip could take an hour and fifteen minutes every weekday.

You might recognize the name Snouffer from Snouffer School Road near Montgomery Village. The road was named after his distant relative George Snouffer, who once donated an acre of his land for a school to be built in Gaithersburg.

Before it became a mecca for mansion hunters, Potomac was a quieter country community. Ben was a toddler when his family got electricity. His father worked as a painting contractor, and his mother, Emma, did all the housework. "Mama helped to do some cooking; Daddy used to cook too," he reminisced. "Everything was fried: fried chicken, fried ham, fried pork chops. I never had anything other than fried food until I was an adult—it was a porterhouse steak."

As a kid, some of Ben's favorite activities included going to Glen Echo Park with family and friends, attending a country dance at the Cabin John Fire Hall and cranking up his family's Victrola radio to listen to music from the Grand Ole Opry. He hunted ducks, swam and fished along the Potomac River at Swain's Lock, a local hangout spot with a refreshment stand. One of Ben's childhood classmates was Fred Swain, whose family was the lock's namesake.

While Ben enjoyed his youth on the Potomac River, it was not without hardship. One day in 1955, his father, Joseph, went out to work on Ben's sister Mary Jane's car, a 1941 Ford coupe, in the driveway of their home. When sixteen-year-old Ben came up the driveway from school that day, he discovered that his father had become the victim of a freak accident. The car had somehow rolled back onto Joseph Snouffer, fatally pinning him.

Ben Snouffer as a boy with his toy plane, circa 1949. *Ben and Diana Snouffer.*

With the patriarch of the family gone, young Ben stepped up to support his family. He worked as a painter with his brother Harry Joe before pursuing and earning a full-fledged apprenticeship in his senior year of high school. "Apprenticeships covered plumbing, woodworking, machinists, electricians, modelmakers: blue-collar tradesmen," Mr. Snouffer said. "The apprentice exam was an eight-hour exam down at Washington Navy Yard. It covered math, science and English."

In 1956, Ben Snouffer began working in Carderock, Maryland, at the David Taylor Model Basin (DTMB), which is known today for being one of the largest naval testing facilities in the world. While at the DTMB, he achieved two major accomplishments. For one, he got to create wooden models for ships and technology to be used by the U.S. Navy. And secondly, he got the chance to meet his future wife, Diana Stone, who was in charge of signing out the design plans. The two got to know each other better through a duckpin bowling league that the basin held every Wednesday night. "She used to walk through my woodshop on the way to the cafeteria. One time, I asked her to come dancing with me, and that's how it got started," Mr. Snouffer said.

Snouffer left his job at Carderock in 1966 to work on exhibits for the Smithsonian museums in Washington. For this fascinating new job, he made full-size clay and Styrofoam horses to exhibit at the Postal History Museum. He worked with taxidermists to get real horsehair and manes to make his models more lifelike.

For another project, he put together an exhibit to honor Ben Abruzzo, Maxie Anderson and Larry Newman, the three men who, in 1978, piloted the *Double Eagle II*, which became the first hot air balloon to successfully cross the Atlantic Ocean. As part of his job, Snouffer worked to obtain the life masks of the men to create his models. "I made a lot of astronauts too," he said. "I made face molds of Native American children in New Mexico, the legs and hands and feet out of Jeltrate. That's what dentists make molds out of."

Today, eighty-five-year-old Ben Snouffer is retired and lives in rural Dickerson, Maryland, with Diana, his wife of almost sixty years and the mother to their two children. He is an active churchgoer and golfer, crediting his faith and his active lifestyle with how he has lived into his mid-eighties. While much of his career took place in the city, Mr. Snouffer feels most at home far away from it. He said:

> *This part of Montgomery County is special to us; I've been here all my life. I wouldn't want to live in New York City. Anywhere out in the country, that's where I want to be.*

# MRS. FRANCES MILLS

On a "beautiful warm Sunday morning," February 7, 1932, Albert and Madeline Young welcomed their daughter, Frances Louise, into the world. Born at home in Dickerson, Frances Young (later Mills) would be the couple's only child, despite the fact that her mother was seventeen years old at the time of her birth. Albert and Madeline married young but ultimately had a long and happy union.

During World War II, Albert traveled around the country for work, promoting a missile made by the Johns Hopkins Applied Physics Laboratory. He brought Madeline a collectible plate from each state he visited, and today, Mrs. Frances Mills has kept all forty-eight of them. The Youngs did not have much money, but they tried their best not to let that interfere with their daughter's happiness.

Rounding out the Young household was Madeline's mother, Caroline Roberts. In 1930, she had made the brave decision to separate from her abusive husband, and she eventually became a live-in caretaker for Mills. Caroline became a grandmother at thirty-two, having given birth to Madeline at just fifteen years old. "My grandmother was my playmate," Mrs. Mills said. "She was with me all the time, giving Mother all the time to clean. I was really close with my grandma, and sometimes I thought she was my real mother."

When Frances was six years old, the family moved from Dickerson to Darnestown. On her first day at Darnestown Elementary School, she experienced the gamut of emotions but formed a sacred bond with a girl named Anna Curtis. "During recess, we were scared to death of playing with other kids. So we bonded over our mutual scaredness," Frances recollected. "She's my most favorite friend. We grew up, and her kids played with my son."

High school would bring another important person into her life: her future husband. At first, riding the bus to school in Gaithersburg, she thought she had found him in a boy from Quince Orchard who wrote her love notes. Then one day, she got a note from him that was addressed to another girl. She wasn't the only sweetheart in his life: another girl on the bus got her note.

Welp, Frances got mad. She started sitting on the bus next to one of his neighbors, a boy named Merle Mills, to make the two-timer jealous. "Merle was interesting," Frances Mills said. "He started biking up to date me, then he would drive up to date me. And then we were dating ever since."

Twenty-year-old couple Frances and Merle Mills on their wedding day, September 13, 1952. The ceremony took place at Darnestown Presbyterian Church. *Frances Mills.*

Much unlike his wife, Merle was number eleven in a family of twelve children, many of whom went on to be plumbers. Merle was a handy individual, a plumber by trade who built the house in Darnestown where his wife has lived for more than seventy years. He also became an accomplished pig racer. Traveling up and down the East Coast, he and his pigs gained recognition in many local newspapers and magazines for their efforts on the track. In addition to pigs, the Millses have had dogs, cats and a duck, named Fred after their neighbor.

As much as the Millses loved animals, they also loved children. Frances Mills's career was always driven by her desire to work around them. She applied and was accepted into the Maryland State Teachers College (now Towson University) but was distraught to find out that her parents couldn't afford her tuition. Her father used his political connections to land her a job assisting Alfred D. Noyes, a judge at the Montgomery County Juvenile

Court. "I loved it, just dearly loved it, and I worked there nearly twenty years," Mrs. Mills said. "I would take down notes in the courtroom; that was extremely interesting."

Frances Mills's job with Judge Noyes touched her on a personal level. In one case she still remembers, a mother and grandmother brought their boy to the court and simply left him there. Experiences like this one pushed Frances and her husband toward adopting a child and starting their own family.

The adoption process would not be an easy one for the couple. Frances and Merle Mills were both nearing forty years old. An unwritten rule, forty was once widely considered the cutoff age for agencies to consider someone as an adoptive parent. But when Mrs. Mills was thirty-eight, they finally got to bring home their little four-month-old, Mark Edward. "He was the best little boy," she beamed. "Merle adored him. Whenever he and Mark took off in the car, he would tell him, 'Hang on, boy!' He called him 'boy' so often that Mark came up to me and asked, 'Does Daddy know my name?'"

Over the course of her life, Frances Mills has worked at several MCPS schools, performed a litany of roles with her church and even survived a battle with breast cancer. In her late sixties, she finally left work with Montgomery County Public Schools to help with the care of her new granddaughter. Mrs. Mills is the longest-serving member of Darnestown Presbyterian Church, having joined in 1942 at the age of ten. When she turned ninety, the congregation came together and threw her a birthday party: a "whoop-de-doo," as she affectionately remembers it.

Today, Frances Mills is ninety-two years old. Her husband, Merle, passed away in 1999, but she spends almost every day with her son, Mark; daughter-in-law, Pamela; and granddaughter, Tori. When I interviewed her, she stated that she is most proud of her wonderful family, full of kind, grateful and appreciative people.

When I asked her to reflect on her life in Darnestown, she had this to say:

> *It's very rewarding; you see lots of change. It's difficult, especially with the technology we have now, but it's rewarding and I don't want to leave yet; I've got things to do. I've been up and down the East Coast and up to Alaska. Maybe I'd go to Hawaii. But I'm content. Darnestown's my favorite place.*

## Mrs. Ida Pearl Green

Before I begin this story, I recommend also reading the book *The Making of a Pearl* by Dr. Kisha Davis, the subject's granddaughter, and watching the PBS documentary *Finding Fellowship* by Dr. Davis and her brother Jason Green. These works offer abundant personal insights into the life and community of the siblings' grandmother, Ida Pearl Green. Much of the following biographical information comes from Dr. Davis's book.

Ida Pearl Hallman, better known as Pearl Green, was born on June 18, 1918, in a house on Riffle Ford Road in Quince Orchard. It was a turbulent time: Americans were fighting overseas in World War I, and a flu pandemic affected hundreds of millions of people. However, Pearl Green remembers it as a typical one. "My childhood was pretty much the same as those around us, I think," she said. "We went to church on Sunday mornings and on Sunday evenings had prayer time at home. Mother would read to us from a red book called *Miss Charlotte's Stories of the Bible*."

Pearl Green had a large family, with five younger brothers and two younger sisters. They all attended the Quince Orchard Colored School like their mother, Evelyn, and her siblings before them. Pearl's father, Samuel Hallman, had come from the historically Black community of Martinsburg, Maryland, west of Poolesville. "Things I remember from my childhood are playing games like ring-around-the-rosy and dodgeball with neighborhood children. We would meet up with others and all walk to school," Mrs. Green recalled.

The house where Pearl Green grew up has since been torn down, but the housing development that now stands in its place is called Hallman Court after her family. Long ago, it was the place where the Hallmans lived primarily off the land. "We raised or grew all our food," Pearl said. "I liked turkey, chicken, duck, homemade root beer, milk, apple cider, pears, apples, plums, grapes and all vegetables."

As Mrs. Green puts it in *The Making of a Pearl*, she had "a good childhood filled with love but also with pain." As a poor Black family during the Great Depression, the Hallmans faced many health and financial challenges. Both Green and her baby brother Upton faced life-threatening illnesses. Upton Hallman survived a severe case of whooping cough, while Green nearly lost her foot when a mysterious illness attacked it. In 1934, her twelve-year-old brother Sam contracted acute meningitis, and despite the family's best efforts to find him treatment, he succumbed to the illness. Pearl learned from her mother to rely on faith and prayer when dark times arose.

Pearl's mother, Evelyn, was a dedicated saleswoman. When her husband, Pearl's father, lost his job, Evelyn went around to neighbors selling chamber pots for a living. The White women of Quince Orchard recognized her talent, and many of them hired Evelyn to sell their goods at the market because of how profitable she was.

Rather than coming to the door and introducing her product right away, Evelyn Hallman would start a casual, friendly conversation with the customer. Sometimes, they invited her in for a visit, and often, Evelyn convinced them to buy a chamber pot. Pearl would follow in her mother's footsteps to become a door-to-door saleswoman later in life. Frances Mills, who volunteered at Quince Orchard High School, fondly

Ida Pearl Green as a young woman, circa 1940. *Kisha Davis and Rita Green.*

remembers meeting Mrs. Green when she visited the school to sell Avon beauty products.

Mrs. Green has been married twice: first to Howard Bell, then to Gerard Green. Howard and Pearl married in 1938, leading her to move briefly to the Black neighborhood of Lincoln Park in Rockville. While she hadn't noticed it much in Quince Orchard, Green realized in Rockville that segregation was all around her. She and her husband usually had to "go around the back" when they wanted to enter a movie theater or eat at a restaurant.

In one passage of *The Making of a Pearl*, Mrs. Green recalls waking up one night very disturbed, six months pregnant with their first child. Rousing Howard awake, she explained that she had dreamed they were driving along Route 240 (now Route 355) and a car pulled out in front of them, killing Howard. He consoled her, telling her there was nothing to worry about, and the two went back to bed.

The following Monday, October 28, 1940, it happened. As they were driving down Route 355, a car made an illegal turn in front of them. Howard lost control of the car. Pearl and her baby survived, but Howard didn't. This was a major turning point in her life. Rather than sinking deep into her grief, she resolved to push through the tragedy in order to care for her son, "Little" Howard, who was born the following February. She came back to Quince Orchard and married again in 1948, to Gerard Green. They were married until his passing in 1991 and had two sons together, Gerard Jr. and Vernon.

If you lived in Quince Orchard in the 1960s like Pearl Green did, you saw a lot of change happen quickly. There was the police brutality toward civil rights marchers and the assassination of John F. Kennedy. In December 1963, beloved local shopkeeper Donald Snyder was murdered. Fueled by rumors that Snyder was rich, a man from Silver Spring came into the store, shot Snyder in the back of the head and stole less than one hundred dollars from the cash register. Pearl remembers Snyder as a White man who treated both Black and White children in Quince Orchard equally, offering his general store as a center for the community.

The year 1968 would be a defining one for Quince Orchard. There was a vote on the table about whether the three struggling Methodist churches in the area should merge to save themselves from financial ruin. On April 4 that year, the assassination of Martin Luther King Jr. devastated the community's Black residents and made Green realize that the churches needed to come together. As two White churches, McDonald Chapel and Hunting Hill, and one Black church, Pleasant View, they would be fulfilling King's dream of integrating both races. The motion to merge ultimately passed, and the three churches came together to form Fairhaven United Methodist Church, which remains a diverse and lively congregation today. The McDonald Chapel and Hunting Hill Methodist Churches no longer exist, but Pleasant View Methodist Church still sits along Darnestown Road across from the Kentlands neighborhood.

At 105 years old, Pearl Green has gone from a poor girl attending the Quince Orchard Colored School to a learned semi-supercentenarian who can say she has met the first Black President of the United States. She has cruised the Caribbean and peered into the Grand Canyon. When she was 79, her son and grandson baptized her in the Jordan River. She has a big, tight-knit family, including a brother who just turned 100, and is proud to call Montgomery County her home. "I'm most proud of my 60-plus years of selling Avon," Mrs. Green said. "And I'm most proud of all three of my kids graduating from high school."

When I asked her how someone might get to be 105 years old, she offered me the following mantra: "Keep living!"

# BIBLIOGRAPHY

## Books

Barrow, Healan, and Kristine Stevens. *Olney: Echoes of the Past*. Westminster, MD: Willow Bend Books, 2000.

Bicentennial Commission. *Our Bicentennial Cookbook*. Edited by Mary Esta Mosley. Damascus, MD: Damascus Publishing, 1976.

Blair, Gist. *Annals of Silver Spring*. Washington, DC: Columbia Historical Society, 1918.

Boyd, Thomas H.S. *The History of Montgomery County, Maryland: From Its Earliest Settlement in 1650 to 1879*. Baltimore, MD: W.K. Boyle & Son, 1880.

Buglass, Ralph. *Rockville*. Charleston, SC: Arcadia Publishing, 2020.

Cohen, Anthony Michael. *The Underground Railroad in Montgomery County, Maryland: A History and Driving Guide*. Rockville, MD: Montgomery County Historical Society, 1997.

Coleman, Margaret Marshall. *Montgomery County: A Pictorial History*. Norfolk, VA: Donning, 1990.

Cook, Richard, and Deborah Lange. *Glen Echo Park: A Story of Survival*. Glen Echo, MD: Bethesda Communications, 2005.

Curtis, Shaun. *Around Gaithersburg*. Charleston, SC: Arcadia Publishing, 2020.
———. *Gaithersburg*. Charleston, SC: Arcadia Publishing, 2010.

Cuttler, Dona L. *The History of Clarksburg, King's Valley, Purdum, Browningsville and Lewisdale* [MD]. Bowie, MD: Heritage Books, 2001.
———. *The History of Comus*. Bowie, MD: Heritage Books, 1999.

————. *The History of Dickerson, Mouth of Monacacy, Oakland Mills, and Sugarloaf Mountain* [MD]. Bowie, MD: Heritage Books, 1999.

Cuttler, Dona L., and Dorothy J. Elgin. *The History of Poolesville*. Bowie, MD: Heritage Books, 2000.

Cuttler, Dona L., and Michael Dwyer. *The History of Hyattstown*. Bowie, MD: Heritage Books, 1998.

Davis, Kisha N. *The Making of a Pearl*. North Potomac, MD: EKD Mind Body, 2023.

Dwyer, Michael. *Montgomery County*. Charleston, SC: Arcadia Publishing, 2006.

Edwards, Philip K. *Washington Grove 1873–1937: A History of the Washington Grove Camp Meeting Association*. Washington Grove, MD: self-published, 1988.

Farquhar, Roger Brooke. *Historic Montgomery County, Maryland: Old Homes and History*. Brookeville, MD: American History Research Associates, 1952.

Frye, Ethel Gardiner. *Wilson Wims: A Remarkable Life*. Self-published, 2014.

Gagne, Sally. *North Hills of Sligo Creek: History, People and Surroundings*. Silver Spring, MD: self-published, 2003.

Goetz, Walter A. *Montgomery County Gold Fever*. Bethesda, MD: self-published, 1988.

Grazulis, Thomas P. *Significant Tornadoes: 1680–1991—A Chronology and Analysis of Events*. St. Johnsbury, VT: Tornado Project of Environmental Films, 1993.

Henson, Josiah, and John Lobb. *Uncle Tom's Story of His Life: An Autobiography of the Rev. Josiah Henson, 1789–1876*. London: Cass, 1971.

Jaffeson, Richard C. *Silver Spring Success: The 300-Year History of Silver Spring, Maryland*. Silver Spring, MD: self-published, 2003.

Jewell, E. Guy. *From One Room to Open Space: A History of Montgomery County Schools from 1732 to 1965*. Rockville, MD: Montgomery County Public Schools, 1976.

Lampl, Elizabeth Jo, and Kimberly Prothro Williams. *Chevy Chase: A Home Suburb for the Nation's Capital*. Crownsville, MD: Maryland Historical Trust Press, 1998.

Lottes, Karen Yaffe, and Dorothy Pugh. *In Search of Maryland Ghosts: Montgomery County*. Atglen, PA: Schiffer, 2012.

MacMaster, Richard K., and Ray Eldon Hiebert. *A Grateful Remembrance: The Story of Montgomery County, Maryland*. Rockville, MD: Montgomery County Historical Society, 2013.

Manakee, Harold R. *Indians of Early Maryland*. Baltimore, MD: Maryland Historical Society, 1969.

Markwood, Louis N. *The Forest Glen Trolley and the Early Development of Silver Spring.* Arlington, VA: National Capital Historical Museum of Transportation, 1975.

Marsh, Ellen R., and Mary Anne O'Boyle. *Takoma Park: Portrait of a Victorian Suburb, 1883–1983.* Takoma Park, MD: Historic Takoma, 1984.

McDaniel, George W. *Black Historical Resources in Upper Western Montgomery County.* Barnesville, MD: Sugarloaf Regional Trails, 1979.

McGuckian, Eileen S. *Historic and Architectural Guide to the Rockville Pike.* Rockville, MD: Peerless Rockville Historic Preservation, 1995.

McGuckian, Eileen S., and Lisa A. Greenhouse. *F. Scott Fitzgerald's Rockville: A Guide to Rockville, Maryland, in the 1920s.* Rockville, MD: Peerless Rockville Historic Preservation, 1996.

Mhley, Rita Rammrath. *Woodmont Country Club: A History.* Rockville, MD: Woodmont Country Club, 1988.

Montgomery County Historical Society. *We the People: Montgomery County and the Constitution.* Rockville, MD: self-published, 1988.

Myers, Brian. *Greater Than a Tourist: Gaithersburg, Maryland, USA.* Lock Haven, PA: CZYK Publishing, 2020.

Offutt, William M. *Bethesda: A Social History.* Bethesda, MD: Innovation Game, 1996.

Oordt, Darcy. *Haunted Maryland: Dreadful Dwellings, Spine-Chilling Sites, and Terrifying Tales.* Guilford, CT: Globe Pequot, 2016.

Palmer, Laura-Leigh. *Wheaton.* Charleston, SC: Arcadia Publishing, 2009.

Prince, Bryan. *A Shadow on the Household: One Enslaved Family's Incredible Struggle for Freedom.* Toronto: Emblem/McClelland & Stewart, 2010.

Ritter, T.J., and Alice Gitchell Kirk. *The People's Home Library: A Library of Very Practical Books.* Cleveland, OH: R.C. Barnum, 1913.

Soderberg, Susan Cooke. *A History of Germantown, Maryland.* Germantown, MD: self-published, 1988.

Still, William. *Underground Railroad Records: Narrating the Hardships, Hairbreadth Escapes, and Death Struggles of Slaves in Their Efforts for Freedom.* Philadelphia, PA: Porter & Coates, 1872.

Sween, Jane C., and William Offutt. *Montgomery County: Centuries of Change: An Illustrated History.* Sun Valley, CA: American Historical Press, 1999.

Walston, Mark. *Montgomery County.* Charleston, SC: Arcadia Publishing, 2011.

Welles, Judith. *Cabin John: Legends and Life of an Uncommon Place.* Cabin John, MD: Cabin John Citizens Association, 2008.

———. *Potomac.* Charleston, SC: Arcadia Publishing, 2019.

## Newspapers and Periodicals

*Alexandria (VA) Gazette*
*Baltimore (MD) Sun*
*Chicago Defender*
*Evening Star* (Washington, DC)
*Frederick (MD) News-Post*
*Maryland Gazette* (Annapolis, MD)
*Montgomery County (MD) Sentinel*
*Montgomery (MD) Journal*
*New York Times* (New York, NY)
*Sunday Herald* (Washington, DC)
*Washington Post*
*Washington Times*

## Other Sources

Acanfora, Joe. "A Gay Teacher's Battle to Teach." Joe Acanfora: Gay History, 2006. https://joeacanfora.com.

American Meteorological Society. "Severe Local Storms, May 1929." *Monthly Weather Review* 57, no. 5 (1929). https://doi.org/10.1175/1520-0493(1929)57%3C216:SLSM%3E2.0.CO;2.

Ancestry. https://www.ancestry.com.

Andersen, Patricia Abelard. "The Almshouse, Later Called the 'County Home,' 1789–1948: A History of Poor Relief in Montgomery County." *Montgomery County Story* 41, no. 2 (May 1998).

Anonymous. "Triadelphia: The Three Brothers." *Religious Telescope* 77, no. 34 (August 23, 1911). http://patuxentwatertrail.org/public_html/patuxentwatertrail.org/wp-content/uploads/2013/04/Triadelphia_History.pdf.

Aronson, Janet Krasner, Matthew A. Brookner, Matthew Boxer and Leonard Saxe. "2017 Greater Washington Jewish Community Demographic Study." Jewish Data Bank, March 21, 2018. https://www.jewishdatabank.org/api/download/?studyId=1093&mediaId=bjdb%5c2017_Greater_DC_Jewish_Study_Summary_Report.pdf.

Blair Alumni. *Silverlogue 1946.* Silver Spring, MD: Montgomery Blair High School, 1946. https://www.blairalumni.org/wp-content/themes/universh-child/images/PDF/Silverlogue/1946.pdf.

Browne, Allen. "The Cabin John Bridge." *Landmarks* (blog), May 1, 2011. https://allenbrowne.blogspot.com/2011/05/cabin-john-bridge.html.

Browne, Allen C. "A Real Field of Dreams." Edited by Bill Pfingsten. Historical Marker Database, September 22, 2019. https://www.hmdb.org/m.asp?m=95723.

Butler's Orchard. "About Butler's Orchard." https://www.butlersorchard.com/about/about_butlers.

CBS. "The Case of Joe Acanfora on CBS' *60 Minutes*." YouTube, June 26, 2022. Uploaded by Joe Acanfora. Video, 15:35. https://www.youtube.com/watch?v=G1JvUnFjB4E.

City of Gaithersburg. https://www.gaithersburgmd.gov.

Cook, Richard A. "A General History of Glen Echo Park." Glen Echo-Cabin John Area History, December 2008. https://glenecho-cabinjohn.com/GE-04.html.

Crane, Brian. "The Poor Farm Cemetery: A Dark and Overlooked Part of Our Past." The Third Place (*blog*), March 3, 2021. https://montgomeryplanning.org/blog-design/2021/03/the-poor-farm-cemetery-a-dark-and-overlooked-part-of-our-past.

Crook, Mary Charlotte. "Hyattstown, A Roadside Town Preserved." *Montgomery County Story* 29, no. 2 (May 1986).

Damascus Heritage Society Museum. https://dhsm.org.

Davis, Jason, and Kisha Davis. *Finding Fellowship*. PBS, February 1, 2022. Video, 57:14. https://www.pbs.org/video/finding-fellowship-3bz18O.

Defandorf, Harriet, and Mayvis Ellis Fitzsimons. "Memories of Garrett Park." *Montgomery County Story* 16, no. 3 (August 1973).

Diamond, Jillian. "Born the Same Year as Israel, Ohr Kodesh Congregation Celebrates 75th." *Washington Jewish Week*, May 10, 2023. https://www.washingtonjewishweek.com/born-the-same-year-as-israel-ohr-kodesh-congregation-celebrates-75th.

Dwyer, Michael F., and Harry T. Bussard. "Meeting with Mr. Harry T. Bussard and His Grandchildren at the Farmhouse." M-NCPPC, May 12, 1977.

Dwyer, Michael F., and Mary Lawson Bussard. "Phone Conversation with Mrs. Harry T. Bussard." M-NCPPC, May 9, 1977.

———. "Phone Conversation with Mrs. Harry T. (Lawson) Bussard." M-NCPPC, February 17, 1977.

Fierst, Edith. "Oral History Interview with Flora Singer." United States of America: Holocaust Eyewitness Project, 1988. https://collections.ushmm.org/search/catalog/irn39562.

Find a Grave. https://www.findagrave.com.

Ford, Jane. "The Story of 'Uncle Tom's Cabin' Spread from Novel to Theater and Screen." *UVA Today*, November 12, 2012. https://news.virginia.edu/content/story-uncle-tom-s-cabin-spread-novel-theater-and-screen.

Founders Online. https://founders.archives.gov.

Fourth Presbyterian School. "The Fourth Presbyterian School: Home." 2012. https://web.archive.org/web/20120310090923/http://www.fourthschool.org.

Gaithersburg Community Museum. https://www.gaithersburgmd.gov/about-us/city-facilities/gaithersburg-community-museum.

Gartner, Jeanne. *Reed Brothers Dodge History 1915–2012* (blog). https://reedbrothersdodgehistory.com.

George, Elise. "Our Illustrious History." Browningsville Cornet Community Band. https://www.browningsvillecornet-communityband.org/history.

Heritage Montgomery. "Life in a War Zone: A Guide to the Civil War in Montgomery County, Maryland." October 2015. https://www.heritagemontgomery.org/wp-content/uploads/2015/10/civil-war-brochure.pdf.

Higgins, Dora B. "Letter of Dora Higgins [to Sophia C. Barnard]." Peerless Web Exhibit: The Civil War Comes to Rockville. Peerless Rockville, 2006. http://tigger2.us/CWExhibit/pages/HigginsLetter.htm.

History.com Editors. "Fugitive Slave Acts." History.com, December 2, 2009. https://www.history.com/topics/black-history/fugitive-slave-acts.

Hoffmann, Melane Kinney. "Legacy Family Farming Is Alive and Well in MoCo's Ag Reserve: Three Generations of Butlers Reflect the Evolution of Family Farming." *Plenty*, 2023.

Jewish Federation of Greater Washington. "Maryland." JConnect, September 23, 2019. https://www.jconnect.org/resources/new-to-the-area/maryland.

Johnson, Hannah. "Silver Spring's Jewish History 'Long and Complicated.'" *Washington Jewish Week*, November 10, 2017. https://web.archive.org/web/20210523054523/https://www.washingtonjewishweek.com/silver-springs-jewish-history-long-and-complicated.

Kiger, Patrick. "Rachel Carson in Silver Spring." Boundary Stones, August 15, 2023. https://boundarystones.weta.org/2017/01/19/rachel-carson-silver-spring.

Library of Congress. https://loc.gov.

Maryland Historical Trust. https://mht.maryland.gov/Pages/default.aspx.

Maryland Land Records. https://mdlandrec.net.

Maryland National-Capital Park and Planning Commission. https://www. mncppc.org.

Maryland State Archives. "Emily Edmonson." Maryland Women's Hall of Fame, 2009. https://msa.maryland.gov/msa/educ/exhibits/ womenshallfame/html/edmonson.html.

MedStar Health. "The Women's Board: MedStar Montgomery Medical Center: Medstar Health." 2023. https://www.medstarhealth.org/ locations/medstar-montgomery-medical-center/about-our-hospital/the-womens-board.

MoCoCouncilMD. "Did You Know—Behind the Names of Places—Sam Eig Highway." YouTube. December 4, 2014. Video, 5:46. https://www. youtube.com/watch?v=lahOXNfnOxo.

———. "Paths to the Present: Montgomery County Stories: Browningsville Cornet Band (Paths #70)." YouTube. February 9, 2017. Video, 7:10. https://www.youtube.com/watch?v=A7oHHeJ94R8.

———. "Paths to the Present: Montgomery County Stories: Walking Tour of Garrett Park & Montgomery Connections History Project." YouTube. May 5, 2015. Video, 15:01. https://www.youtube.com/ watch?v=-jr6jn-pQJw.

Montgomery County District Council. "Cedar Grove Historic District Amendment Map, 1990." https://montgomeryplanning.org/wp-content/uploads/2019/09/Cedar-Grove-HD-Amendment-Map.pdf.

Montgomery County Historical Society. https://montgomeryhistory.org.

Montgomery-National Capital Park & Planning Commission.

National Oceanic and Atmospheric Administration. "The Fujita Scale." National Weather Service, August 15, 2018. https://www.weather.gov/ ffc/fujita.

National Park Service. "Chautauqua Era." October 12, 2017. https:// www.nps.gov/glec/learn/historyculture/chautauqua-era.htm.

———. "A Summer of Change: The Civil Rights Story of Glen Echo Park." August 3, 2021. https://www.nps.gov/glec/learn/historyculture/ summer-of-change.htm.

The People's Archive, MLK Library. https://thepeoplesarchive.dclibrary. org/repositories/2.

Roberson, Mike, and Adam Froehlig. "495 Vintage Gallery." Virginia Highways Project, 2015. http://www.vahighways.com/495vintage/ index.htm.

Sandy Spring Museum. https://www.sandyspringmuseum.org.

Segraves, Mark. "Co-Writer of 'Take Me Home, Country Roads' Dispels Myths Surrounding Song's Origins." NBC4 Washington, December 31, 2020. https://www.nbcwashington.com/news/local/co-writer-of-take-me-home-country-roads-dispels-myths-surrounding-songs-origins/2525010.

Spivack, Miranda S. "The Not-Quite-Free State: Maryland Dragged Its Feet on Emancipation during Civil War." *Washington Post*, September 13, 2013. https://www.washingtonpost.com/local/md-politics/the-not-quite-free-state-maryland-dragged-its-feet-on-emancipation-during-civil-war/2013/09/13/a34d35de-fec7-11e2-bd97-676ec24f1f3f_story.html.

Storm Prediction Center, Russell S. Schneider, Harold E. Brooks, and Joseph T. Schaefer, 12 § (2004). https://www.spc.noaa.gov/publications/schneider/otbrkseq.pdf.

Thomas, Craig. "Farm Transition and Succession—Why Bother?" MSU Extension, July 29, 2021. https://www.canr.msu.edu/news/farm_transition_and_succession_why_bother.

Town of Washington Grove. "History of Washington Grove." 2021. https://washingtongrovemd.org/about-wg/our-history/history-of-washington-grove.

U.S. EPA. "DDT: A Brief History and Status." April 3, 2023. https://www.epa.gov/ingredients-used-pesticide-products/ddt-brief-history-and-status.

United States Memorial Holocaust Museum. https://www.ushmm.org.

Walston, Mark. "The Growth of the Jewish Community in Montgomery County." *MoCo360*, February 21, 2022. https://moco360.media/2022/02/20/the-growth-of-the-jewish-community-in-montgomery-county.

Walston, Mark, and Zazelle Bussard Royer. Interview with Mrs. Zazelle Bussard Royer. October 5, 1979.

Walston, Mark, and Zazelle Royer. Further Conversations with Mrs. Zazelle Royer. October 15, 1979.

Watts, Alden, Edith Bussard Cross and Debbie Cross Lee. "Transcript of Conversation with Mrs. Edith Bussard Cross and Mrs. Debbie Cross Lee." Montgomery County Parks Department, May 8, 2008.

WBNS-TV Staff. "Vowels in Some Street Signs Removed to Prevent Theft in Maryland County." 10 WBNS, December 22, 2019. https://www.10tv.com/article/news/nation-world/vowels-some-street-signs-removed-prevent-theft-maryland-county-2019-dec/530-508ab478-78d5-4f7a-ac69-03386b60328a.

Wyrauch, Kevin. "Glen Echo on the Potomac." YouTube. January 20, 2013. Video, 58:58. https://www.youtube.com/watch?v=LatpnwBBxEs.

# INDEX

## A

Acanfora, Joseph "Joe"  60, 62, 65, 66
Agricultural Historical Farm Park  150, 153
Alexandria  22, 105
American Revolution, the  13, 18
Anacostan tribe  13
Aspen Hill  102
Aspin Hill Pet Cemetery  101, 105
Atzerodt, George  40

## B

Baltzley, Edwin and Edward  109
Bannockburn civil rights protests  112
Barnesville  25, 37
Battle of Ball's Bluff, the  36
Beale, Priscilla  24
Beallsville  23, 138
Beecher, Henry Ward  47

Bentley, Caleb  32
Bethesda  59, 112, 130, 171, 180
Billy the Litter Eater  127
Bird, Dr. Jacob W.  48, 88, 94
Black Hill Regional Park  100
Blair, Montgomery  40
Blair Witch Experience, The  137
*Blair Witch Project, The*  131
Blazi, Matt  134, 139
Bolton, James "Jim"  92, 94
Boyds  171
Braddock, Gen. Edward  15
Briggs, Isaac  32
Briggs, Samuel and Lelia  81
Brighton Dam  35
Brinklow  49
Brooke, Roger and Mary  32
Brookeville  15, 32, 38, 56, 83, 84, 85, 91, 120
Brookmont  80
Brookside Gardens  128
Browningsville  121, 157
Browningsville Band  121

Bussard
  Ann Priscilla  150
  Eleanor  78
  Harry Sr.  153
  Thaddeus Tyson  150
Butler family, the  143
Butler's Orchard  81, 143, 146, 148

**C**

Cabin John  185
Cabin John Regional Park  127
Cafritz, Morris  68
Carderock  186
Carson, Rachel  54
Cecil, Hammedatha and Mary Ann
      169
Chandler's wobble  176
Chautauqua movement, the  109,
      116
Chesapeake Bay  13
Chevy Chase  68
Childs, F. Bowie  85
Cider Barrel  144
Civil Rights Movement  112, 192
Civil War  25, 34, 40, 81
Claggettsville  38
Clara Barton  109
Clara Barton House  109
Clarksburg  15, 57, 58, 120, 150
Clopper Road  164
Colesville  161
Congregation Ohr Kodesh  68
Connelly, Jessie  77
Coolidge, Calvin  105
cornet bands  120
cotton  33
county home. *See* poor farm

**D**

Damascus  120, 154, 157
Danoff, Bill  164
Darnestown  23, 137, 181, 187, 189
Darnestown Elementary School
      187
Darnestown Presbyterian Church
      189
David Taylor Model Basin  186
DDT  54
Denver, John  164
Derwood  81, 163
DeSellum, John and Sarah  38
Dickerson  23, 159, 186, 187
Douglass, Frederick  47
Dove, William  159
Dowden's Ordinary  15
drummer boy  80
Duvall, Trovilla  77

**E**

Early, Gen. Jubal  38
Earp, John  91
Edmonson, Mary and Emily  45
Eig, Samuel "Sam"  68, 124
Eisenhower, Dwight D.  52
Emory Grove  119

**F**

Fair Housing Act, the  68
Falkland  40
Fleet, Henry  13
Ford, Gerald R.  164
Fourth Presbyterian Church  180
Fourth Presbyterian School  180

Franklin, Benjamin  15
Frederick  67
Fugitive Slave Acts, the  43

## G

Gaithersburg  38, 56, 70, 78, 95,
        116, 119, 125, 179, 184, 187
Gaithersburg Latitude Observatory
        176
Garrett Park  172
Georgetown  20, 111, 164
Georgetown College. *See*
        Georgetown University
Georgetown University  20
Germantown  40, 81, 90, 92, 95,
        100, 133, 143, 144, 161
ghosts  80, 83
Glen Echo  109, 111
Glen Echo Park  111, 112, 114,
        115, 185
Glenmont  161
gold rush  169
Great Falls  13, 170
Green, Ida Pearl  190
Grosvenor, Gilbert H.  161
Gude, Gilbert  163

## H

Henson, Josiah  13, 83
Higgins, Dora  37
Hilton, William T.  25
Holocaust, the  70
Hoover, J. Edgar  105
Humpback Bridge  119
Hungerford, Charles  18
Hungerford's Tavern  18

Hunting Hill  192
Hurley, Fr. Leonard  161
Hyattstown  57, 90
Hyattstown Bluebirds  58

## J

Jackson, Andrew  18
Jewish families  68

## K

Kay, Abraham S.  68
Kennedy
    Jacqueline "Jackie"  128
    John F.  56, 161, 192
    Robert F.  114, 124
Kent, Otis  159
King, Martin Luther, Jr.  192

## L

Lansdale, Thomas  33
Lawrence, Helen  78
Layhill  77
Laytonsville  38, 68, 84, 85, 159
liquor  36
Little Bennett Regional Park  57, 83
Little Falls  80

## M

Madison, James  33
Magruder, Zadok  18
    Zadok  151
Maryland Gold Mine  170
Maryland Wildcats  57
Mason, Geneva  159

McDonald Chapel  192
Mercer
  John Francis  24
  Sophia Sprigg  24
Metropolitan Branch  116, 119, 172
Miles, Mayor Richard H.  78
Mills, Frances  187, 189
Montevideo  23
Montgomery County Agricultural
    Reserve  26, 146
Montgomery County General
    Hospital  48, 50, 88, 93, 94
Montgomery General Hospital  153
Montgomery, Gen. Richard  18
Montgomery Village  184
Moore, Thomas  32
Myrick, Daniel  132

**N**

Neelsville  78, 98
Negro league baseball  58
neighborhoods
  Anacostia  47
  Avondale  65
  Bannockburn  112
  Brickyard  160
  Cedar Grove  157
  Emory Grove  160
  Good Hope  160
  Grifton  85
  Hoyles Mill Village  160
  Indian Spring  68
  Kemp Mill  68
  Kentlands  159, 192
  King's Valley  120
  Lincoln Park  58, 191
  Manor Oaks  163
  Quaint Acres  54

Redland Park  163
Rock Creek Forest  68
Scotland  58, 159
Seven Oaks  144
Slidell  67
Travilah  120
Woodfield  154
Woodside  75
Newmantown  151
Nivert, Mary Catherine "Taffy"
    164
Norbeck  68
North Bethesda  44, 45
North Potomac  160
Noyes, Alfred D.  188

**O**

Olde Towne Gaithersburg. *See*
    Gaithersburg
Olney  161, 163
Owen's Ordinary  15, 18

**P**

Parkland Junior High School  60
Patuxent River  32, 34, 85
*Pearl* incident, the  47
Penn, William  77
Peter
  Martha Parke Custis  23
  Thomas  23
Piscataway tribe  13
Pleasant View  192
Poolesville  37, 68, 120, 166
poor farm  28
Porky the Litter-Eating Pig  127
Potomac  71, 120, 159, 171, 180,
    184

Potomac River  13, 36, 80, 109, 160, 185
Povich, Maury  63
Prospect Hill  15

**Q**

Quince Orchard  187, 191, 192
Quince Orchard Colored School  190

**R**

recipes  154
Redland  77
Revolutionary War  80
Richter, Hartman  40
Robertson, John and Clara  98
Rockville  18, 31, 35, 44, 56, 58, 62, 68, 85, 95, 171, 176, 182, 191
Rockwell, George Lincoln  114
Rosenstein, Louis and Dora  67
Roxbury Mills  85
Rye Cove tornado outbreak, the  84, 88

**S**

Sánchez, Eduardo  131, 139
Sandy Spring  35, 47, 48, 49, 52
Sandy Spring Friends Meetinghouse  76
Seneca  23
Seneca Creek  77, 136, 137
Seneca Creek State Park  133, 137
Shady Grove Hospital  31
Shady Grove Music Fair, the  70, 124
Shaw, Lacey  30

Shelley v. Kraemer (1948)  68
Sherwood Academy  35
Sherwood High School  51
Shipley
  Douglass  91, 92, 99
  Hattie  91, 93, 99
Silent Spring  54
Silver Spring  40, 54, 71, 75, 143, 166, 192
Singer, Flora Mendelowicz  70
slavery  36, 43, 47
Smith
  Capt. John  13
  Edwin  176
Snouffer
  Benjamin G. "Ben"  184, 186
  George  184
Snouffer School  184
Snyder, Donald  192
Spanish-American War, the  91
Spanish influenza epidemic  50
Sprigg family, the  172
Sprigg, Thomas, Jr.  24
St. Martin's School  184
Stowe, Harriet Beecher  45
Stuart, Gen. J.E.B.  37
Suburban Hospital  31
Summit Hall  38
Swain's Lock  185

**T**

"Take Me Home, Country Roads"  164
Takoma Park  54, 78, 131
Thompson
  Dewey  98
  Guy Vernon  90, 93, 94, 95, 98
  Hester Earp  91, 93, 95, 98

tobacco 15, 20, 25
Triadelphia 32, 33, 34
Triadelphia Bell 35
Triadelphia Lake 32, 35
Tschiffely
  Elgar 160
  Frederick Jr. 159
  Frederick Sr. 159
  Wilson 160
typhoid fever 173

## U

*Uncle Tom's Cabin* 45
Underground Railroad, the 43, 45,
    47
Unity 91

## W

War of 1812, the 33
Washington, D.C. 47, 62, 67, 70,
    80, 102, 116, 119, 186
Washington, George 15, 23, 27, 83
Washington Grove 116, 119, 120
Washingtonian Country Club 70
Washington Sanitarium 78
Washington Suburban Club. *See*
    Woodmont Country Club
Waters' Mill 90, 92, 94, 100
Weems, Ann Maria 45
Wheaton 68, 128, 131
Wheaton Regional Park 127
Whetstone Branch 116
Williams, Earl Larkin 177
Wilson, Woodrow 68
Wims, Wilson 57, 59
Woodmont Country Club 68

Woodstock 23, 25, 83
Wootton, Dr. Thomas Sprigg 18
Wrenwood Hospital 49

# ABOUT THE AUTHOR

B rian Myers graduated from the University of Maryland (UMD) in 2023 and currently works as a business and technology operations analyst. While at UMD, he majored in information systems and marketing and studied screenwriting under three-time Emmy winner Michael Olmert. His first book, a travel guide called *Greater Than a Tourist—Gaithersburg, Maryland*, was published in 2020. He began to study genealogy as an elementary schooler and now has a working family tree of more than twenty-five thousand members. He was born in Rockville and raised in Gaithersburg, Maryland, where he still lives with his parents—but not for too much longer. You can sometimes catch him as the cowbell guy in the UMD-based band the Skill Issues.

*Visit us at*
www.historypress.com
·······································································